Soulcon Warrior 365 Devotional

365 Days to Forge Faith, Courage, and Spiritual Strength

Cody Bobay

Copyright © 2025 Cody Bobay
All rights reserved.
ISBN: 9798281878449

1 CORINTHIANS 16:13-14
"BE ON YOUR GUARD; STAND FIRM IN THE FAITH; BE COURAGEOUS; BE STRONG. DO EVERYTHING IN LOVE."
ESV

CONTENTS

Dedication i

1 Intro 1

2 Day 1-365 All Pgs

DEDICATION

To the warriors who have completed *The Soulcon Challenge*—
I honor you.
You didn't just read a book.
You stepped into a battle.
You chose discipline over comfort.
Conviction over compromise.
Faith over fear.
You said yes to a call that many ignore—
to be a man marked by sacrifice, strength, and spiritual grit.
This devotional exists because of men like you—
men who chose to rise at dawn,
get uncomfortable,
embrace accountability,
and live out their faith with fire in their bones.
Your courage has built this brotherhood.
Your example has inspired countless others to stand up and step in.
Your walk has helped reignite what it means to be a warrior for Christ.
Thank you for being part of this mission.
Thank you for refusing to live a passive life.
And thank you for reminding the world what a man of God really looks like.
This 365-day devotional is for you—
a daily war plan for a man who's already stepped onto the battlefield
and refuses to retreat.
Keep rising. Keep fighting. Keep leading.
Until we breathe our last breath or hear the trumpet sound,
we stand together—swords drawn, shields locked, eyes up.

For the King,
Cody Bobay
Founder of Soulcon

GALATIANS 2:20
"I HAVE BEEN CRUCIFIED WITH CHRIST. IT IS NO LONGER I WHO LIVE, BUT CHRIST WHO LIVES IN ME AND THE LIFE I NOW LIVE IN THE FLESH I LIVE BY FAITH IN THE SON OF GOD, WHO LOVED ME AND GAVE HIMSELF FOR ME."
ESV

Introduction

Before diving in, I want to encourage you to download the Soulcon App and join thousands of men from around the world just like you. It's free and it's a powerful community of Christian men living on the front lines...

Welcome to the Front Lines

this isn't just a devotional.
This is a war manual.

You won't find soft sentiment or sugar-coated spirituality in these pages. What you'll find is a call—loud and clear—for men to rise. To fight. To stand in the gap. To lead with integrity. To reject passivity. To pursue Jesus with the heart of a warrior and the discipline of a soldier.

If you're reading this, it means something inside you refuses to live a lukewarm life. You've felt the tension between who you are and who you're called to be. You've heard the whispers of heaven and the growls of hell—and you've decided not to sit on the sidelines.

Good.

Because this devotional is built for men who are ready to live differently. Every day is a full-page war plan:

- A powerful quote from a Christian leader to spark your fire.

- A bold message from God to your warrior heart.

- A Scripture to ground you.

- A daily challenge to put your faith into action.

- A warrior's prayer to sharpen your soul.

You don't need perfection to walk through this. You need grit, humility, and holy defiance. You need the willingness to show up, suit up, and fight your battles with truth, love, and spiritual fire.

This world is desperate for godly men.
Men who don't fold under pressure.
Men who repent quickly, rise stronger, and lead fiercely.
Men who look like Jesus in a culture that looks like chaos.

That's why this exists.

You've got 365 days ahead of you.
365 chances to be forged.
365 chances to become the man God made you to be.

Welcome to the Soulcon Warrior Brotherhood.
You were born for this.

Now grab your sword.
And let's begin.

Cody Bobay

January 1

"Resolution one: I will live for God. Resolution two: If no one else does, I still will."
Jonathan Edwards

Son,
this year doesn't need more goals—
it needs more grit.
More resolve.
More obedience at all costs.

You don't need a clean slate—
you need a consecrated spirit.
The world doesn't need more noise from believers—
it needs more warriors who live like their lives belong to Me.

Start this year with fire, not fluff.
With conviction, not comfort.
With a decision so deep hell flinches when your feet hit the ground.

Even if no one else follows—
you will.

"As for me and my house, we will serve the Lord."
— Joshua 24:15

Daily Challenge: Write down one resolution: *"This year I will live for God, no matter the cost."* Say it aloud. Sign it in ink.

Warrior's Prayer:
Father, this year is Yours. All of it. I lay down every excuse and pick up my cross. Even if I walk alone, I will walk with You. Make this year the fiercest yet for Your Kingdom. In Jesus' name, Amen.

January 2

"The difference between who you are and who you want to be is what you do."
Craig Groeschel

Son,
you weren't created to coast.
Growth doesn't come through good intentions—
it comes through holy discipline.

You can't drift into greatness.
You must choose it daily,
train for it fiercely,
and fight for it relentlessly.

It's not enough to want to change.
You must move.
You must build.
You must go to war with your laziness, your excuses, and your comfort zones.

You were made to grow stronger—
in mind, in body, in spirit.

"Train yourself to be godly." — 1 Timothy 4:7

Daily Challenge: Pick one area of your life—faith, fitness, or focus—and create a simple daily training habit. Start today.

Warrior's Prayer:
Father, I will not drift through this life. I choose discipline over comfort. Train me like a soldier. Shape me like a son. I commit to growing stronger through daily faithfulness. In Jesus' name, Amen.

January 3

"A man is no fool who gives up what he cannot keep to gain what he cannot lose."
Jim Elliot

Son,
you cannot keep the praise.
You cannot keep the trophies.
You cannot keep the money.
The status.
The spotlight.

But you can gain something
untouchable.
Eternal.
Unshakable.

Trade the temporary.
Give it up freely.
Cling only to what death cannot steal.

You are no fool
to burn bright now
so others can find the Light forever.

You are My son.
Spend your life boldly.
You'll never regret it.

"Whoever loses their life for Me will find it."
— Matthew 16:25

Daily Challenge: Identify one thing you've been clinging to—release it to God today in prayer and obedience.

Warrior's Prayer:
Father, I let go of the things that will fade. I want to live for what can't be taken—Your glory, Your mission, Your Kingdom. Help me trade what I can't keep for what lasts forever. In Jesus' name, Amen.

January 4
"When you kill time, remember it has no resurrection."
A.W. Tozer

Son,
you don't get today back.
Every hour is a weapon—
wield it with purpose.

Don't waste your life scrolling, coasting, or waiting for the "right time."
This is the time.
This is the war.
This is your shot.

The enemy doesn't have to destroy you—
he just has to distract you long enough to derail you.

Redeem the time.
Every moment you give Me multiplies.
Every second you aim with purpose sends shockwaves into eternity.

"Be very careful, then, how you live—not as unwise but as wise, making the most of every opportunity."
— Ephesians 5:15–16

Daily Challenge: Audit your time today. Replace one time-wasting habit with something that builds your faith or mission.

Warrior's Prayer:
Father, help me stop wasting time on things that don't matter. Teach me to number my days and live with urgency. I want every second of my life to be a weapon in Your hands. In Jesus' name, Amen.

January 5

"Hardships often prepare ordinary people for an extraordinary destiny."
C.S. Lewis

Son,
I know it hurts.
The weight. The waiting. The wilderness.

But don't waste the hard.
I'm not punishing you—
I'm preparing you.

Pressure isn't the enemy—
it's the forge.
It's where warriors are shaped,
where kings are crowned in secret.

You are not being buried—
you're being built.

Hold the line.
Your pain has a purpose.
Your scars will one day shine with My glory.

"Consider it pure joy... whenever you face trials of many kinds, because you know that the testing of your faith produces perseverance." — James 1:2–3

Daily Challenge: Write down one hardship you're facing—and declare over it: "This is preparing me, not defeating me."

Warrior's Prayer:
Father, thank You for using every hardship to shape me. Forge me in the fire. Make me stronger through pressure. I trust You to use every scar to prepare me for the destiny You've designed. In Jesus' name, Amen.

January 6
"We are not called to be successful, but faithful."
Mother Teresa

Son,
the scoreboard the world uses means nothing in My Kingdom.
I don't measure by results—
I measure by obedience.

You're not called to impress—
you're called to endure.
You're not called to perform—
you're called to persevere.

Faithfulness in obscurity
echoes louder in Heaven than fame in the spotlight.

Keep showing up.
Keep obeying.
Keep trusting Me with the outcomes.

Well done starts with still showing up.

"Now it is required that those who have been given a trust must prove faithful." — 1 Corinthians 4:2

Daily Challenge: Be faithful today in something small—show up, follow through, and do it as worship.

Warrior's Prayer:
Father, teach me to be faithful, not flashy. I give You the pressure to perform and choose obedience instead. Help me keep showing up, trusting You with the results. In Jesus' name, Amen.

January 7
*"When you understand that life is a test, you
realize nothing is insignificant."*
Rick Warren

Son,
nothing in your day is wasted.
Not the interruptions.
Not the long waits.
Not even the suffering.

Every moment is an opportunity to respond with faith,
to grow in grit,
to trust deeper.

I use traffic jams to build patience.
I use detours to develop character.
I use silence to strengthen your dependence.

Don't despise the small moments.
They are the proving grounds of your calling.

"Whoever can be trusted with very little can also be trusted with much..." — Luke 16:10

Daily Challenge: Treat every moment today—especially the frustrating ones—as a test of your faith. Pass it with purpose.

Warrior's Prayer:
Father, help me see every moment as sacred. Even the interruptions. Even the slowdowns. Use each test to train me for greater responsibility. In Jesus' name, Amen.

January 8

"A true soldier fights not because he hates what is in front of him, but because he loves what is behind him."
G.K. Chesterton

Son,
you are not fueled
by rage.
You are fueled
by love.

You fight
because you remember the cost.
You endure
because you've been called
to protect more than yourself.

The mission is bigger
than your mood.
The battle is deeper
than today's pressure.

Fight for your family.
Fight for the broken.
Fight for the man you're becoming.

Let love be your fire.
Let eternity be your reason.
You are not just surviving—
you are defending legacy.

"Greater love has no one than this: to lay down one's life for one's friends." — John 15:13

Daily Challenge: Remind yourself who and what you're fighting for today—write it down, declare it, and carry it into every action.

Warrior's Prayer:
Father, let love fuel my fight today. Help me to remember that every sacrifice I make in obedience is for Your Kingdom and for those You've placed under my care. Make me a defender, not just a doer. In Jesus' name, Amen.

January 9

"The greatest tragedy is not death, but life without purpose."
Myles Munroe

Son,
you were not born to blend in.
You were born to break chains.

I didn't breathe life into you
so you could live safe,
build comfort,
and die quietly.

You carry purpose in your bones—
fire in your soul.

Every day you live disconnected from your calling
is a day you give the enemy ground.

Stop surviving.
Start advancing.
I made you for mission.

"Before I formed you in the womb I knew you, before you were born I set you apart..." — Jeremiah 1:5

Daily Challenge: Write out your mission—what you believe God created you to do—and take one step toward it today.

Warrior's Prayer:
Father, awaken Your purpose in me again. Shake off the apathy. Kill the distractions. Align my life with Your mission and send me into this day like a man with fire in his soul. In Jesus' name, Amen.

January 10

"You can't fulfill your calling in isolation. You need the strength of the brotherhood."
John Eldredge

Son,
lone wolves don't last in battle.
You were never meant to fight alone.

I wired you for brotherhood—
for shared burden,
shared prayer,
shared war.

The enemy's first strategy is isolation.
Because a man without a brother
is an easy target.

Drop the pride.
Drop the silence.
Lean into the fire of brotherhood—
and become unshakable together.

"Two are better than one... If either of them falls down, one can help the other up." — Ecclesiastes 4:9–10

Daily Challenge: Reach out to a brother in Christ today. Encourage, pray, or confess. Build strength together.

Warrior's Prayer:
Father, keep me from isolation. Surround me with brothers who sharpen me, strengthen me, and call me higher. Make me a man who fights shoulder-to-shoulder in the Kingdom army. In Jesus' name, Amen.

January 11
"God does not call the qualified; He qualifies the called."
A.W. Tozer

Son,
you don't need a perfect résumé to walk in purpose.
You don't need applause to have authority.

I'm not calling you because you're ready.
I'm calling you because you're willing.

I've always chosen the underqualified, the broken, the overlooked.
Why?
Because I get the glory.
Because no one can say it was their strength.

So stop disqualifying yourself.
I already called you.
That's enough.

"Brothers and sisters, think of what you were when you were called. Not many of you were wise by human standards..." — 1 Corinthians 1:26

Daily Challenge: Step into one area of obedience today where you've felt unqualified. Trust God to equip you as you go.

Warrior's Prayer:
Father, I lay down every excuse and insecurity. If You've called me, You'll equip me. I walk forward not because I'm ready, but because You are with me. In Jesus' name, Amen.

January 12
"Only in surrender to Jesus do we find true freedom"
Watchman Nee

Son,
freedom isn't free—
and neither is your calling.

If you want to live unchained,
you'll have to die to comfort.
If you want to live as a warrior,
you'll have to bleed for the battle.

You were not made to live soft.
You were made to live surrendered.
And surrendered men walk into war without turning back.

Freedom is yours—
but it's carried on the shoulders of sacrifice.

"Take up your cross daily and follow Me." — Luke 9:23

Daily Challenge: Identify one area where comfort is keeping you from obedience—and kill it today with action.

Warrior's Prayer:
Father, I choose the cross over comfort today. I want freedom more than ease. Make me willing to die to anything that keeps me from living fully for You. In Jesus' name, Amen.

January 13

"The devil fears a man who fears only God."
Leonard Ravenhill

Son,
fear no man.
Fear no demon.
Fear no failure.

Bow only to Me.

When you fear Me,
you walk in unshakable peace.
When you fear Me,
the enemy trembles when you pray.

I am the Lion behind your roar.
The Shield over your name.
The Fire in your bones.

Live holy.
Live bold.
Live like you kneel before no throne but Mine.

"The fear of the Lord is the beginning of wisdom."
— Proverbs 9:10

Daily Challenge: Face today with fearless faith—declare: "I fear God, so I fear nothing else."

Warrior's Prayer:
Father, burn out every fear that doesn't belong. I want to walk with holy reverence and fearless obedience. Make me a man who bows only to You and stands firm in every storm. In Jesus' name, Amen.

January 14
*"Obedience is the burial of pride beneath
the soil of surrender."*
Charles Stanley

Son,
obedience isn't glamorous—
but it is powerful.

It's not about feeling like it.
It's about following through.
You don't obey because you always understand—
you obey because you trust Me more than you trust yourself.

Every time you obey,
you're planting seeds in the ground.
Seeds that will become strength, victory, and legacy.

Obedience is the battlefield where pride dies and purpose is born.

"If you love Me, keep My commands." — John 14:15

Daily Challenge: Obey immediately today in one area you've been hesitating. Don't delay—move.

Warrior's Prayer:
Father, crush the pride in me that resists surrender. Give me the courage to obey quickly, fully, and joyfully. I trust You more than I trust my feelings. In Jesus' name, Amen.

January 15
"You find out what you're made of when the fire hits."
Eric Ludy

Son,
talk is cheap when the battlefield is quiet.
The fire reveals who's real.

When the heat rises,
the false melts.
The faithful stand.

You don't grow strong by avoiding the fire—
you grow strong by walking through it with Me.

The furnace doesn't destroy you—
it reveals you.

So stop fearing the fire.
Embrace it.
Because every trial is a forge—
and you're being refined, not ruined.

"When you walk through the fire, you will not be burned; the flames will not set you ablaze." — Isaiah 43:2

Daily Challenge: When pressure hits today, declare: "This fire is forging me."

Warrior's Prayer:
Father, walk me through the fire. Don't let me waste the heat. Refine me, purify me, and use the pressure to shape a faith that lasts. I will not flinch—I will be forged. In Jesus' name, Amen.

January 16

*"Let God have your life; He can do
more with it than you can."*
Dwight L. Moody

*Son,
I'm not asking for a part of your life.
I want the whole thing.*

*Not just your Sundays—
your secrets.
Not just your prayers—
your plans.
Not just your sin—
your ambition.*

*I don't want control because I'm a tyrant.
I want it because I'm the only one who sees the full map.*

*What you keep from Me becomes your greatest risk.
What you give to Me becomes your greatest strength.*

"In all your ways acknowledge Him, and He will make your paths straight." — Proverbs 3:6

Daily Challenge: Surrender one area of your life today you've been holding back—trust God fully with it.

Warrior's Prayer:
Father, I give You not just the pieces of my life, but the whole. I trust Your hands more than mine. Lead me, shape me, and have it all. In Jesus' name, Amen.

January 17
"One person with courage is a majority."
Thomas Jefferson

Son,
I don't need an army to shift history.
I just need one man fully surrendered.

The world changes when one warrior stands.
When one voice speaks.
When one life refuses to bow.

You plus My Spirit is more than enough.

Don't wait for consensus.
Don't look for a crowd.
If I've called you—stand.

I've always used the few to ignite the many.

"Be strong and courageous. Do not be afraid... for the Lord your God goes with you." — Deuteronomy 31:6

Daily Challenge: In one situation today, choose to lead with courage—even if no one else steps forward.

Warrior's Prayer:
Father, I don't need to be popular—I need to be faithful. Fill me with courage to stand when others stay silent. Let my life be a spark for something greater. In Jesus' name, Amen.

January 18

"There is no such thing as a secret sin. It always leaks into your legacy."
Paul Washer

Son,
sin hides in shadows,
but it poisons the whole house.

What you refuse to kill
will eventually kill your fire.
What you justify in secret
will rot your strength in public.

There are no harmless secrets.

Drag it into the light.
Expose the enemy.
Confess it.
Crush it.

Your legacy depends on your honesty.

I already paid for it—
so stop protecting what I came to destroy.

"Have nothing to do with the fruitless deeds of darkness, but rather expose them." — Ephesians 5:11

Daily Challenge: Confess one hidden sin today to a brother in Christ. Don't hide—get free.

Warrior's Prayer:
Father, I refuse to protect the sin You died to destroy. Give me the courage to drag darkness into the light. Purify my legacy. I want nothing hidden, nothing fake. In Jesus' name, Amen.

January 19

"A man who won't die for something is not fit to live."
Martin Luther King Jr.

Son,
your life gains value
when it's attached to something bigger than you.

When you live only for self,
you shrink.
When you live for Me,
you rise.

I'm calling you to something worth dying for.
A mission that makes demons tremble.
A cause that echoes in eternity.

Don't waste your days stacking comfort.
Spend them laying down your life for others,
for truth,
for My Kingdom.

This is how you live fully—
by being willing to give it all.

"For to me, to live is Christ and to die is gain." —
Philippians 1:21

Daily Challenge: Today, serve someone sacrificially—not for applause, but as an offering to God.

Warrior's Prayer:
Father, I want to live for something worth dying for. Let every breath I take be spent for You. Make me bold enough to give everything, not just what's easy. In Jesus' name, Amen.

January 20
"Character is who you are in the dark."
D.L. Moody

Son,
your reputation is what people see—
your character is who you are when no one's watching.

The real war isn't out there—
it's in the silence.
In the decision no one applauds.
In the moment when no one will know—except Me.

What you do in the dark determines what you carry in the light.

Be the same man in secret as you are on stage.
Be the same warrior when no one's watching.
I see.
I reward.
I refine.

"The integrity of the upright guides them, but the unfaithful are destroyed by their duplicity."
— Proverbs 11:3

Daily Challenge: Choose integrity today when no one's looking. Make one choice that honors God in secret.

Warrior's Prayer:
Father, build in me a character that stands, even when no one sees. Forge integrity deep in my bones. Let me be the same man in the shadows as I am in the spotlight. In Jesus' name, Amen.

January 21

"If you want to know what a man's like, take a good look at how he treats his inferiors, not his equals."
J.K. Rowling

Son,
true strength isn't measured by how you lead the powerful—
but how you serve the overlooked.

The world honors the loud, the rich, the visible.
But I watch how you treat the unseen.

Every interaction is a test of character.
The waiter.
The janitor.
The broken.

If you want to be a great man,
start by being a humble one.

The greatest warriors carry towels, not just swords.

"Whoever wants to become great among you must be your servant." — Matthew 20:26

Daily Challenge: Serve someone today who can do nothing for you in return—and do it quietly.

Warrior's Prayer:
Father, strip away my pride. Help me lead with humility and serve with love. Teach me to see the invisible and treat every person as someone made in Your image. In Jesus' name, Amen.

January 22

"It is not your business to succeed, but to do right. When you have done so, the rest lies with God."
C.S. Lewis

Son,
outcomes are My job—
obedience is yours.

You don't have to control the results.
You don't have to manipulate the numbers.
You don't have to fight for credit.

You just need to do what's right.
Even when it's hard.
Even when it costs you.

Righteousness isn't always rewarded in this life.
But I see.
And I reward with what truly matters.

"Trust in the Lord and do good... commit your way to the Lord; trust in Him and He will act." — Psalm 37:3–5

Daily Challenge: In one situation today, do what's right—even if it doesn't benefit you.

Warrior's Prayer:
Father, help me choose integrity over results. Teach me to trust You with outcomes and stay faithful in obedience. Let my actions reflect Heaven even when no one else does. In Jesus' name, Amen.

January 23

*"Worry does not empty tomorrow of its sorrow—
it empties today of its strength."*
Corrie ten Boom

Son,
worry lies.
It tells you you're in control.
It whispers that fear keeps you prepared.

But worry
is a thief.

It steals your peace.
It weakens your walk.
It blinds you to what I'm already doing.

You cannot fight well
with a mind full of fear.

You cannot lead boldly
while rehearsing every worst-case scenario.

Lay it down.
Trust Me with tomorrow.
Take back your strength
for today.

"Do not worry about tomorrow, for tomorrow will worry about itself. Each day has enough trouble of its own." — Matthew 6:34

Daily Challenge: When anxiety rises today, stop and declare: "I won't borrow fear—I choose faith."

Warrior's Prayer:
Father, I release the weight of worry. I trust You with what I can't control. Fill my mind with truth and my heart with courage. Today is Yours—I will walk in faith. In Jesus' name, Amen.

January 24

*"The best measure of a spiritual life is not
its ecstasies but its obedience."*
Oswald Chambers

Son,
spiritual highs are great.
But I'm not looking for emotion—
I'm looking for endurance.

Goosebumps fade.
Obedience lasts.

You prove your maturity
not by how high you jump in worship,
but by how faithfully you walk on Tuesday morning.

Don't chase moments—
build momentum.
I want your heart,
your habits,
your hidden places.

Live grounded.
Live steady.
Live surrendered.

"Blessed are those who hear the word of God and obey it." — Luke 11:28

Daily Challenge: Choose consistency over emotion today—pray, serve, or worship even if you don't *feel* it.

Warrior's Prayer:
Father, I choose steady obedience over emotional hype. Build in me a disciplined faith, rooted in Your truth. Let my life be shaped by surrender, not sentiment. In Jesus' name, Amen.

January 25
*"The greatness of a man's power is in the
measure of his surrender."*
William Booth

Son,
you don't grow stronger by grabbing more—
you grow stronger by giving Me more.

The world says power comes from control.
But Kingdom power flows from surrender.

The more you yield,
the more I fill.
The more you release,
the more I release through you.

Total surrender isn't weakness—
it's the gateway to unstoppable strength.

Let go.
Open your hands.
I will do more with your surrender
than you could ever do with your control.

"Not my will, but Yours be done." — Luke 22:42

Daily Challenge: Surrender one area of control you've been holding tightly—pray it out loud and release it today.

Warrior's Prayer:
Father, I lay it all down. My future, my plans, my fears—I surrender it to You. Take control. Lead me deeper into the strength that comes through surrender. In Jesus' name, Amen.

January 26

*"The greatest use of a life is to spend it for
something that will outlast it."*
William James

Son,
this life is a mist.
Short. Fragile. Gone in a blink.

But your impact doesn't have to vanish.
You were made to leave a trail of eternal fire.
Souls touched.
Truth spoken.
Generations changed.

Don't burn time chasing what rusts.
Invest your days in what no thief can steal.

Every sacrifice you make for My Kingdom echoes forever.

Spend your life well, son.
Spend it bold.

"Store up for yourselves treasures in heaven... for where your treasure is, there your heart will be also." — Matthew 6:20–21

Daily Challenge: Ask God where your life is invested—and shift one part of your day toward something eternal.

Warrior's Prayer:
Father, teach me to number my days and to use them for what lasts. Let my life be spent, not saved. I want to invest every breath in eternity. In Jesus' name, Amen.

January 27

"The strength of a man's soul is measured by how much truth he can bear."
Dallas Willard

Son,
truth is heavy.
But it's what sets men free.

Don't settle for watered-down sermons or convenient lies.
Dig for the truth.
Swallow it whole,
even when it stings.

Truth convicts before it liberates.
It breaks before it builds.

But I promise—
if you anchor your life to truth,
you'll be unshakable.

You weren't built to carry lies.
You were born to bear truth,
speak truth,
and fight for truth.

"Then you will know the truth, and the truth will set you free." — John 8:32

Daily Challenge: Read a passage of Scripture today that convicts you—don't skip it, let it shape you.

Warrior's Prayer:
Father, make me a man of truth. Even when it's hard. Even when it hurts. Help me to bear it, speak it, and live it. Anchor me to what is real and unshakable. In Jesus' name, Amen.

January 28

"Don't shine so others can see you. Shine so that through you, others can see Him."
C.S. Lewis

Son,
you were never meant
to be the source of the light—
you are the reflection.

Every gift,
every victory,
every moment you shine—
is a mirror of My glory.

Don't crave the spotlight.
Crave the presence.

The world doesn't need more stars.
It needs more torches.
Burn bright,
not for applause,
but for direction.

Shine to lead.
Shine to reveal Me.
Shine with a fire
that leaves no doubt
who your Father is.

"Let your light shine before others, that they may see your good deeds and glorify your Father in heaven." — Matthew 5:16

Daily Challenge: In one conversation or post today, make the focus not about you—but all about Jesus.

Warrior's Prayer:
Father, I don't want the credit—I want to reflect You. Use my life to shine Your truth, grace, and love into every dark place I enter. In Jesus' name, Amen.

January 29
"All great change begins at the dinner table."
Ronald Reagan

Son,
revival doesn't just happen in stadiums—
it starts in your home.

The table matters.
The way you lead, pray, listen, and love
when no spotlight's around—
that's the real battlefield.

You don't need a microphone to make an impact.
You need consistency.
Presence.
Conviction.

If you want to change the world—
start with your wife.
Start with your kids.
Start with your table.

"But as for me and my house, we will serve the Lord." —
Joshua 24:15

Daily Challenge: Initiate prayer, a word of encouragement, or Scripture in your home today—lead from the front.

Warrior's Prayer:
Father, let revival start in my house. Let my table be an altar. Teach me to lead my family not just in public but in the hidden moments. In Jesus' name, Amen.

January 30
"God does not anoint plans—He anoints people."
Leonard Ravenhill

Son,
you don't need a perfect blueprint.
You need a burning heart.

Too many men wait for clarity
instead of seeking intimacy.
Too many build schedules
instead of surrendering fully.

I'm not looking for polished plans—
I'm looking for laid-down lives.

I don't anoint ambition.
I anoint surrender.

The plan will come.
First, become the man.

"You did not choose Me, but I chose you and appointed you..." — John 15:16

Daily Challenge: Spend time with God today not to get direction—but simply to get closer.

Warrior's Prayer:
Father, make me a man You can anoint. Strip away selfish plans. Align my heart with Yours. Use me—not because of my strategy, but because of my surrender. In Jesus' name, Amen.

January 31
"Every man gives his life for what he believes. Sometimes people believe in little or nothing..."
William Wallace

Son,
you are giving your life to something.
Every day.
Every breath.

The question isn't if you're sacrificing—
the question is what for?

Some give their lives to comfort.
Others to image.
Others to nothing at all.

You were made to give your life for something immortal.
Something worthy of blood.
Something that changes eternity.

Live like your life has weight.
Because it does.

"Be steadfast, immovable, always abounding in the work of the Lord, knowing that your labor is not in vain." — 1 Corinthians 15:58

Daily Challenge: Reflect on what you're currently giving your life to—and adjust anything that's not worthy.

Warrior's Prayer:
Father, I want to spend my life on what matters. Let me not waste a single day on the meaningless. Burn away distractions. Aim my life at Your glory. In Jesus' name, Amen.

February 1
"It is not great men who change the world, but weak men in the hands of a great God."
Hudson Taylor

Son,
you don't need to be impressive—
you need to be available.

You don't have to be the strongest, fastest, smartest—
you just have to say "yes."

I've never needed heroes—
I raise up surrendered men and turn them into weapons.

Don't wait to be enough.
You never will be.
But I always am.

Let Me work through you.
And watch the impossible fall.

"But He said to me, 'My grace is sufficient for you, for My power is made perfect in weakness.'"
— 2 Corinthians 12:9

Daily Challenge: Identify one area of weakness—and let God use it today instead of hiding it.

Warrior's Prayer:
Father, I give You my weakness. Use me in ways I cannot imagine. I don't have to be great—I just have to be Yours. Work through me for Your glory. In Jesus' name, Amen.

February 2
"A ship is safe in harbor, but that's not what ships are for."
John A. Shedd

Son,
you weren't saved to play it safe.
I didn't redeem you for the harbor—
I called you to the storm.

Faith doesn't grow in comfort.
It grows in motion,
in risk,
in obedience.

You'll never find your purpose chained to the dock.
Untie the rope.
Lift the anchor.
Push into the deep.

That's where My power meets you.
That's where warriors are made.

"Put out into deep water, and let down the nets for a catch." — Luke 5:4

Daily Challenge: Do something today that feels risky for the Kingdom—step into deep waters by faith.

Warrior's Prayer:
Father, I choose the deep over the dock. I won't settle for safe. Lead me where I need You, where I grow, and where You are glorified. In Jesus' name, Amen.

February 3
"You can't defeat what you won't define."
Craig Groeschel

Son,
the enemy thrives
in the shadows.

Addiction.
Pride.
Lust.
Fear.

If you won't name it,
you can't kill it.

Stop pretending.
Stop hiding.
Stop hoping it fades on its own.

Call it out.
Drag it to the Cross.
Slay it in the open.

Freedom starts
when truth meets courage.

"Confess your sins to each other and pray for each other so that you may be healed." — James 5:16

Daily Challenge: Name your battle today. Say it out loud. Confess it to a brother. The fight starts with the truth.

Warrior's Prayer:
Father, I won't hide what You came to heal. Give me courage to name the battle, confess the sin, and walk in freedom. I'm done with shadows. In Jesus' name, Amen.

February 4

*"Reputation is what men say about you on your tombstone.
Character is what angels say about you before the throne."*
William Hersey Davis

Son,
don't waste your life managing your image.
Build your integrity.

You can fool men.
But Heaven sees everything.

The secret you protect today
becomes the fracture that breaks you tomorrow.
But the character you forge in silence
will roar in eternity.

Don't live for applause—
live for approval.

Mine.

"The Lord does not look at the things people look at. People look at the outward appearance, but the Lord looks at the heart." — 1 Samuel 16:7

Daily Challenge: Make one decision today based on character, not popularity or perception.

Warrior's Prayer:
Father, shape my character in the unseen. Strip away the need to be impressive. Let me live to please You alone. Build in me a heart that reflects Heaven. In Jesus' name, Amen.

February 5
"You will never change what you tolerate."
Mike Huckabee

Son,
what you allow will grow.
What you tolerate will eventually take over.

Compromise doesn't start loud—
it starts subtle.

A second glance.
A silent pass.
A "just this once."

But every time you let it slide,
you let the enemy build a foothold.

Draw the line.
Don't dance with sin.
Kill it early.
Crush it completely.

"Do not give the devil a foothold." — Ephesians 4:27

Daily Challenge: Identify one area of compromise in your life—and shut it down today with bold action.

Warrior's Prayer:
Father, show me where I've allowed sin to linger. Give me strength to cut off every compromise. Make me ruthless with anything that weakens my walk with You. In Jesus' name, Amen.

February 6

"When I really enjoy God, I find my soul so filled with Him that I have no room for sin."
George Müller

Son,
holiness isn't just about avoiding sin—
it's about being filled with Me.

You weren't created to fight temptation with willpower.
You were created to walk in intimacy with Me so strong
that the lesser things lose their pull.

I am not calling you to white-knuckle religion.
I'm calling you to a relationship so deep
that everything else fades in comparison.

Fill your heart, son.
Not with fear—
but with fire.

"Delight yourself in the Lord, and He will give you the desires of your heart." — Psalm 37:4

Daily Challenge: Set aside 15 minutes today to enjoy God's presence—no agenda, just hunger.

Warrior's Prayer:
Father, I want more of You. Let Your presence fill me so deeply that sin loses its grip. Awaken holy passion and joy in You that drives out every lesser desire. In Jesus' name, Amen.

February 7

*"A man's greatest test is not when he fails,
but when he succeeds."*
Oswald Chambers

*Son,
failure tests your grit—
but success tests your heart.*

*When the door opens,
will you stay humble?
When the praise comes,
will you deflect it to Me?*

*The enemy attacks the proud subtly—
by feeding them praise until they forget their Source.*

*Victory doesn't make you untouchable—
it makes you targetable.*

*Stay low.
Stay grateful.
Stay grounded in Me, not the spotlight.*

"Pride goes before destruction, a haughty spirit before a fall." — Proverbs 16:18

Daily Challenge: Give God full credit for a recent success. Speak it aloud. Write it down.

Warrior's Prayer:
Father, I don't want to fall into pride when things go well. Keep me grounded in grace. Remind me that every victory is from Your hand. Make me dangerous to hell because I stay low before You. In Jesus' name, Amen.

February 8

"If you are neutral in situations of injustice, you have chosen the side of the oppressor."
Desmond Tutu

Son,
you were not saved
to be silent.

The moment you turn your face
from injustice—
you turn your back
on the hurting.

Neutrality is not nobility.
It is permission.

I called you
to stand.
To speak.
To confront darkness
even when your voice shakes.

You don't need the full plan—
you just need the fire
to say,
"This isn't right."

Be the voice
that echoes Mine.

"Speak up for those who cannot speak for themselves..." —
Proverbs 31:8

Daily Challenge: Take a stand for someone or something today—even if it's uncomfortable.

Warrior's Prayer:
Father, give me courage to stand where others sit in silence. Let my voice reflect Your justice. Make me a defender of the voiceless, a warrior who stands for truth. In Jesus' name, Amen.

February 9

*"The cost of obedience is nothing compared to
the cost of disobedience."*
Charles Stanley

Son,
obedience always costs something—
comfort, pride, approval.

But disobedience costs more—
peace, power, destiny.

You don't see the full ripple of your obedience—
but I do.
One "yes" today can shift generations.

Don't hesitate when I call.
Delayed obedience is disobedience in disguise.

Say yes.
Even when it hurts.
Even when it's not popular.
Even when you don't see the outcome yet.

"To obey is better than sacrifice..." — 1 Samuel 15:22

Daily Challenge: Obey immediately today in one area God has been prompting—no delay, no excuses.

Warrior's Prayer:
Father, I don't want to pay the price of delayed obedience. I say yes today. Teach me to trust even when I don't fully understand. Let my obedience shape eternity. In Jesus' name, Amen.

February 10

"Hell fears the man who knows who he is in Christ."
John Bevere

Son,
you're not weak.
You're not lost.
You're not barely making it.

You are blood-bought,
Spirit-filled,
and heaven-backed.

The enemy doesn't want you to know that—
because the day you do,
you become lethal.

Walk in your identity.
Don't live like a slave when you've been adopted.
Don't fight like a victim when you've been crowned.

You're not just in the battle—
you're on the winning side.

"The Spirit Himself testifies with our spirit that we are God's children." — Romans 8:16

Daily Challenge: Declare your identity in Christ today. Speak it out loud over your life.

Warrior's Prayer:
Father, I am Yours. I am not my past. I am not my sin. I am a son of the King, sealed by Your Spirit and armed for war. Let me walk in that authority today. In Jesus' name, Amen.

February 11

"The world has yet to see what God can do with a man fully consecrated to Him." — D.L. Moody

Son,
the world is full of half-hearted men.
Half-surrendered.
Half-obedient.
Half-awake.

But I'm looking for the man who goes all in.
Not because he's strong—
but because he's Mine.

Full consecration isn't complicated—
it's complete.

No backup plan.
No reserved areas.
No "God, You can have this, but not that."

The man who gives Me everything
walks with a fire this world can't put out.

"Offer your bodies as a living sacrifice, holy and pleasing to God—this is your true and proper worship." — Romans 12:1

Daily Challenge: Today, write out a full surrender prayer. Nothing held back. Declare it aloud.

Warrior's Prayer:
Father, I hold nothing back. You can have it all—my strength, my story, my scars, my dreams. Make me fully Yours. I want to live with nothing left in reserve. In Jesus' name, Amen.

February 12

"The only thing necessary for the triumph of evil is for good men to do nothing."
Edmund Burke

Son,
evil doesn't win because it's stronger—
it wins when good men stay quiet.

You weren't saved to play defense.
You were saved to take ground.

Passivity is not peace.
It's surrender by silence.

When you see wrong—
speak.
When you see the wounded—
move.
When you see apathy—
burn with purpose.

Do something.
Say something.
Stand for something.

"Do not be overcome by evil, but overcome evil with good." — Romans 12:21

Daily Challenge: Take one bold action today to push back darkness—encourage, confront, or defend.

Warrior's Prayer:
Father, make me a man of action. I will not sit silent while darkness grows louder. Give me courage to stand and the wisdom to know where. In Jesus' name, Amen.

February 13
"God is most glorified in us when we are most satisfied in Him."
John Piper

Son,
you were not made
to chase shadows.
You were made
to be filled.

The world promises joy
but delivers only moments.
The enemy promises life
but hands you chains.

But I give you something deeper.
Joy that stands in storms.
Peace that silences fear.
Purpose that anchors identity.

Find your satisfaction in Me—
not success,
not pleasure,
not applause.

Because when I fill you,
you overflow.

> **"You make known to me the path of life; in Your presence there is fullness of joy..."** — Psalm 16:11

Daily Challenge: Cut out one distraction today and spend that time enjoying God's presence.

Warrior's Prayer:
Father, I've chased lesser things. But today, I turn my heart fully toward You. Satisfy my soul with what is eternal. Let me overflow with Your joy. In Jesus' name, Amen.

February 14

"To love another person is to see the face of God."
Victor Hugo

Son,
real love isn't soft—
it's sacrificial.

It shows up.
It lays down rights.
It carries the weight no one sees.

You were made to love not just with emotion,
but with endurance.

Whether you're married, single, or broken—
the love I've poured into you
is meant to be poured into others.

Start at home.
Start with those closest.
Start with the ones who see your flaws—
and love them like I've loved you.

"Let us not love with words or speech but with actions and in truth." — 1 John 3:18

Daily Challenge: Show intentional love to someone today through sacrifice—not just words, but action.

Warrior's Prayer:
Father, teach me to love like You. Not just when it's easy, but when it costs me. Let my life reflect Your love in real, raw, sacrificial ways. In Jesus' name, Amen.

February 15

"Success is not what you have, but who you become." — Dallas Willard

Son,
you could gain it all—
fame, money, influence—
and still miss the mark.

Because I'm not measuring what you're building—
I'm measuring who you're becoming.

Are you becoming holy?
Are you becoming humble?
Are you becoming strong in weakness
and bold in love?

Success in My Kingdom is measured by transformation,
not titles.

Let Me make you into a man
this world can't ignore—
not because of fame,
but because of fire.

> **"For those God foreknew He also predestined to be conformed to the image of His Son."** — Romans 8:29

Daily Challenge: Spend 5 minutes in silence today and ask God this question: "Who are You making me into?"

Warrior's Prayer:
Father, I want to become more like Jesus. Strip away the parts of me that are still rooted in pride and performance. Shape my soul to reflect Your Son. In Jesus' name, Amen.

February 16

*"Sin will keep you from the Bible, or the Bible
will keep you from sin."*
Dwight L. Moody

Son,
you don't just need My Word when things fall apart—
you need it to stop them from falling.

The battlefield of your mind is won with truth,
not with willpower.
My Word is a sword,
not a slogan.

You're not fighting flesh and blood—
you're fighting lies.
Lies about who you are.
Lies about who I am.

Sharpen your weapon daily.
If you don't feed on truth,
you will be fed by deception.

"Your word is a lamp to my feet and a light to my path."
— Psalm 119:105

Daily Challenge: Read one chapter of Scripture today and write down one truth you'll carry into battle.

Warrior's Prayer:
Father, I don't want to fight unarmed. Burn Your Word into my heart. Let truth be my weapon and my guard. Teach me to wield it with clarity, courage, and conviction. In Jesus' name, Amen.

February 17
"All men die. Not all men really live."
William Wallace

Son,
you were not created to simply exist.
You were made to live with fire.

I didn't save you to survive—
I saved you to move, to fight, to rise.

The world offers distractions,
but I offer purpose.

Every day you wake up without vision
is a day the enemy wins by default.

Breathe deep, son.
Stand tall.
Live fully.
Every moment counts.

> **"I came that they may have life, and have it abundantly."** — John 10:10

Daily Challenge: Do one thing today that stretches your faith, your mission, or your endurance—live fully.

Warrior's Prayer:
Father, wake me up to what matters. Don't let me waste breath on survival when You've called me to live with purpose. Help me burn bright for the Kingdom. In Jesus' name, Amen.

February 18
"The cross is not a decoration—it's a declaration."
John Stott

Son,
the cross is not a symbol of safety—
it's a call to surrender.

It does not invite comfort.
It demands sacrifice.

To carry your cross
is to die to ego,
to bury pride,
to walk where flesh wants to run.

But it is also the place
where death becomes power,
where shame becomes glory,
where surrender becomes strength.

Don't wear the cross.
Carry it.

"Whoever wants to be My disciple must deny themselves and take up their cross daily and follow Me." — Luke 9:23

Daily Challenge: Identify one area of your life where self needs to die—crucify it today through obedience.

Warrior's Prayer:
Father, I pick up my cross today. I lay down pride, comfort, and control. Let the weight of the cross shape me into the image of Christ. I choose the path of surrender. In Jesus' name, Amen.

February 19

*"Your walk talks, and your talk talks—
but your walk talks louder than
your talk talks."*
Leonard Ravenhill

Son,
your actions preach louder than your sermons.

You don't need a pulpit to make an impact.
You just need to live like Jesus is real.

Let your integrity speak louder than your opinions.
Let your faithfulness speak louder than your Instagram.

The loudest men in the room
often lack the power that comes from a quiet life of obedience.

Don't just talk about it—be about it.

"Whatever happens, conduct yourselves in a manner worthy of the gospel of Christ." — Philippians 1:27

Daily Challenge: Let your actions today confirm your faith—especially when no one's watching.

Warrior's Prayer:
Father, make my life louder than my words. Help me live with such integrity that people see You before I say anything. Let my walk declare Your glory. In Jesus' name, Amen.

February 20

"Revival begins when you stop waiting for it to fall and start being the one who brings it."
Leonard Ravenhill

Son,
you are not waiting on revival.
Revival is waiting on you.

It starts with fire in your bones.
It starts with one man broken in prayer,
burning in purity,
walking in obedience.

Don't wait for the crowd—
ignite the spark.

Your hunger matters.
Your repentance matters.
Your worship in the quiet
shakes the gates of hell.

Be the revival.

"Will You not revive us again, that Your people may rejoice in You?" — Psalm 85:6

Daily Challenge: Spend 15 minutes today praying for revival—start with your heart, then your home, then your city.

Warrior's Prayer:
Father, start revival in me. Burn away apathy. Break every barrier. Let my life be the spark that awakens the sleeping. I am available. Send me. In Jesus' name, Amen.

February 21
"There are no crown-wearers in heaven who were not cross-bearers on earth."
Charles Spurgeon

Son,
everyone wants the crown,
but few are willing to carry the cross.

Victory in My Kingdom
doesn't come through applause,
but through endurance.
Through faith in the fire.
Through love when it costs.

You don't get glory without grit.
You don't receive the reward without the road.

Bear your cross.
Walk your path.
I promise—
the crown is worth it.

"If we endure, we will also reign with Him." — 2 Timothy 2:12

Daily Challenge: Endure today without complaining—carry your cross with purpose and perseverance.

Warrior's Prayer:
Father, teach me to carry the cross with faith, not frustration. Let me not grow bitter in the battle. Remind me that suffering for You is never wasted. Crown me with Your presence, not this world's approval. In Jesus' name, Amen.

February 22

*"The devil isn't afraid of a dusty Bible. He's afraid
of the man who lives it."*
Vance Havner

Son,
knowledge without obedience is spiritual dead weight.

It doesn't matter how many verses you can quote
if your life doesn't bleed Scripture.

The enemy doesn't care if you read—
he cares if you respond.

Live the Word.
Move on it.
Apply it in the silence.
Obey it in the resistance.

When you live it,
you don't just carry a sword—
you swing it.

"Do not merely listen to the word, and so deceive yourselves. Do what it says." — James 1:22

Daily Challenge: Choose one verse today and live it—apply it deliberately before the day ends.

Warrior's Prayer:
Father, I don't want to be a man who only knows the Word—I want to be one who lives it. Let my actions prove that Your truth runs deep. Train me to walk, not just read. In Jesus' name, Amen.

February 23

"God is looking for men who are willing to be unpopular if it means being faithful."
Paul Washer

Son,
there is no neutral ground
in a spiritual war.

If you won't stand,
you will be moved.
If you won't plant your feet,
you will drift into compromise.

Draw the line.
Set the standard.
Let your yes mean yes
and your no roar like thunder.

A man of conviction
is a fortress in a world of shifting sand.

> **"Be on your guard; stand firm in the faith; be courageous; be strong."** — 1 Corinthians 16:13

Daily Challenge: Draw one clear boundary today—physically, spiritually, or relationally—and stand firm.

Warrior's Prayer:
Father, make me unshakable in a world full of compromise. Help me draw the lines that guard my purity, purpose, and peace. Teach me to stand firm even when others fold. In Jesus' name, Amen.

February 24
"You don't drift into holiness. You choose it."
Kevin DeYoung

Son,
no one stumbles into strength.
You have to train for it.
You have to choose it.

Holiness is not about perfection—
it's about pursuit.

You won't wake up holy by accident.
You must say no to what's easy
and yes to what's eternal.

This world won't help you.
Hell won't applaud you.
But Heaven will empower you.

Choose holiness today—
and keep choosing it tomorrow.

"Make every effort to live in peace with everyone and to be holy; without holiness no one will see the Lord." — Hebrews 12:14

Daily Challenge: Say "no" to one thing today that dulls your spirit, and "yes" to one thing that sharpens it.

Warrior's Prayer:
Father, I choose holiness. Even when it costs me comfort or approval, I choose to walk in purity and power. Make me holy as You are holy. In Jesus' name, Amen.

February 25

"The man on his knees can see farther than the philosopher on his tiptoes."
Leonard Ravenhill

Son,
vision doesn't come from ambition—
it comes from intimacy.

You don't need another podcast,
another strategy,
another angle.

You need My presence.
You need stillness.
You need clarity that only comes from your knees.

Stop striving.
Start seeking.

I'll show you what matters
when you slow down long enough to listen.

"Call to Me and I will answer you and tell you great and unsearchable things you do not know." — Jeremiah 33:3

Daily Challenge: Spend 10 minutes today in total silence before God. No music. No words. Just listen.

Warrior's Prayer:
Father, I slow down today to hear from You. I need more than inspiration—I need revelation. Teach me to value stillness. Lead me through quiet waters into battle-ready vision. In Jesus' name, Amen.

February 26
*"You may never know that Jesus is all you need
until Jesus is all you have."*
Corrie ten Boom

Son,
the stripping seasons reveal what truly sustains you.
When the comfort fades,
when the crowd leaves,
when the noise quiets—
you find out what you've built your life on.

I am enough.
Not just when things are good—
but when everything else is gone.

If I'm all you have,
you still have more than enough.

Let the world fade.
I will never fail you.

"The Lord is my shepherd; I shall not want."
— Psalm 23:1

Daily Challenge: Identify one area where you've relied on something besides Jesus—lay it down today.

Warrior's Prayer:
Father, if all I have is You, I have everything I need. Strip away every false dependency. Teach me to anchor my soul in Your unchanging presence. In Jesus' name, Amen.

February 27

"It is better to be remembered for standing alone than forgotten for blending in."
John Mason

Son,
I never called you to blend.
I called you to burn.

You weren't made for crowd-pleasing.
You were made to carry conviction.
When everyone else folds,
I want you to stand.

Lions don't follow herds—
they lead them.

Stand alone if you must.
Because when you stand for Me,
you never truly stand alone.

"Do not conform to the pattern of this world, but be transformed by the renewing of your mind."
— Romans 12:2

Daily Challenge: In one moment today, choose conviction over conformity—no matter who's watching.

Warrior's Prayer:
Father, I'd rather stand with You and be judged by the world than stand with the world and be judged by You. Give me the strength to burn bright when I stand alone. In Jesus' name, Amen.

February 28

"God does not give us overcoming life—He gives us life as we overcome."
Oswald Chambers

Son,
victory doesn't fall from the sky.
It's forged through faith.

You don't receive strength
before the battle—
you gain it inside the fight.

Every step forward
is resistance training for your soul.

The breakthrough
is often hidden in the next step of obedience.

Don't wait for ease.
Don't ask for escape.
Ask for endurance.

You were made to overcome.

"Everyone born of God overcomes the world."
— 1 John 5:4

Daily Challenge: Push through resistance today—physically, spiritually, or emotionally. Take one more step.

Warrior's Prayer:
Father, I thank You that I overcome not by avoiding battles, but by walking through them with You. Strengthen me through every step. Give me grit and grace to keep going. In Jesus' name, Amen.

February 29 *(Leap Year Bonus Day)*
*"Live as though Christ died yesterday, rose today,
and is coming back tomorrow."*
Martin Luther

Son,
your days are not infinite.
But what you do with them
can echo forever.

Live like the cross still bleeds.
Live like the tomb just broke open.
Live like the trumpet is about to sound.

No fear.
No hesitation.
No lukewarm living.

This bonus day is a gift—
make it count for eternity.

"Teach us to number our days, that we may gain a heart of wisdom." — Psalm 90:12

Daily Challenge: Treat today like it's your last before Christ returns. Speak boldly. Love deeply. Obey fully.

Warrior's Prayer:
Father, I don't want to waste this day. Thank You for the extra time. Let me use it with urgency, passion, and purpose. If You come back tomorrow, I want to be found burning for You today. In Jesus' name, Amen.

March 1

"Radical obedience to Christ is not easy... It's not comfort, not health, not wealth, and not prosperity in this world. Radical obedience to Christ risks losing all these things. But in the end, such risk finds its reward in Christ. And He is more than enough for us."
David Platt

Son,
obedience isn't about ease—
it's about allegiance.

If you're only willing to follow when it's convenient,
you're not following Me—
you're following comfort.

Radical obedience will cost you:
Comfort. Reputation. Safety.
But it will never cost you joy.

When you risk it all for Me,
you find what truly matters.
And I promise—
I am more than enough.

"Whoever wants to be My disciple must deny themselves and take up their cross and follow Me." — Matthew 16:24

Daily Challenge: Obey God today in one uncomfortable area. Take the risk. Take the step.

Warrior's Prayer:
Father, I want to obey You even when it costs me something. Even when I'm afraid. Even when it doesn't make sense. You are worth everything. In Jesus' name, Amen.

March 2
"Faith that costs nothing is worth nothing."
Leonard Ravenhill

Son,
cheap faith is a lie.
Real faith bleeds.
Real faith moves when logic says stop.
Real faith stands when fear screams run.

If your faith has never cost you anything,
it's time to ask who you're really trusting.

This isn't religion—
this is war.
And your faith is a weapon
meant to strike fear into hell.

Don't settle for a faith that fits in.
Live the kind that breaks chains.

"Without faith it is impossible to please God..." —
Hebrews 11:6

Daily Challenge: Stretch your faith today. Give, speak, or move in a way that costs you something.

Warrior's Prayer:
Father, I don't want a cheap, comfortable faith. I want the kind that shakes the ground and makes darkness tremble. Give me the courage to step out today and trust You completely. In Jesus' name, Amen.

March 3

"The devil's worst nightmare is a man who won't quit – who fears God more than failure."
Tony Evans

Son,
flash fades.
Noise disappears.
But consistency—
that crushes strongholds.

Show up.
Every day.
Even when it's quiet.
Even when no one's clapping.

Hell is not afraid
of your Sunday fire—
it's terrified of your Monday discipline.

You become unstoppable
when you keep showing up
in prayer,
in purity,
in pursuit of Me.

Let consistency be your war cry.

"Let us not grow weary in doing good, for at the proper time we will reap a harvest if we do not give up."
— Galatians 6:9

Daily Challenge: Double down on one discipline today—prayer, Scripture, or service. Don't skip. Lock in.

Warrior's Prayer:
Father, make me consistent. Faithful. Unshakable. Let me be a man who shows up when no one sees, who stays steady when others quit. In Jesus' name, Amen.

March 4
"The blood of the martyrs is the seed of the Church."
Tertullian

Son,
this movement was never built on comfort—
it was built on sacrifice.

Every time you suffer for My name,
you join a line of warriors
who bled for something eternal.

You are not soft.
You are not fragile.
You are part of a bloodline
that does not back down.

I don't waste wounds.
I use them to shake the world.

When you suffer with Me,
you reign with Me.

> **"If we suffer, we shall also reign with Him."**
> — 2 Timothy 2:12

Daily Challenge: Reflect on one moment of hardship in your life—and thank God for how He used it.

Warrior's Prayer:
Father, I embrace the cost of following You. Let my scars speak of Your faithfulness. Use my suffering to strengthen others and to glorify Your name. In Jesus' name, Amen.

March 5

"A dead thing can go with the stream, but only a living thing can go against it."
G.K. Chesterton

Son,
don't be surprised when the current fights you.
That's proof you're alive.

You weren't made to float along.
You were made to swim upstream—
with conviction,
with grit,
with truth.

If your life feels like resistance,
you're probably doing something right.

Keep pushing.
Keep swimming.
You're not drifting—you're advancing.

"Do not be conformed to this world, but be transformed by the renewal of your mind..." — Romans 12:2

Daily Challenge: Make one choice today that pushes against the current of culture—no compromise.

Warrior's Prayer:
Father, give me strength to swim upstream. Make me alive with purpose, filled with courage, and unafraid to stand out. I refuse to float—I will fight. In Jesus' name, Amen.

March 6

"What comes into our minds when we think about God is the most important thing about us."
A.W. Tozer

Son,
your image of Me shapes your entire life.
If you think I'm distant,
you'll stop seeking Me.
If you think I'm angry,
you'll live in shame.

But if you know Me as I truly am—
holy, near, strong, kind, consuming—
you'll live bold, free, and on fire.

You can't walk in victory
while worshiping a distorted vision.

Come close.
Let Me reintroduce Myself.

"Those who know Your name trust in You, for You, Lord, have never forsaken those who seek You." — Psalm 9:10

Daily Challenge: Ask God to reveal one false belief you have about Him—then confront it with truth from Scripture.

Warrior's Prayer:
Father, correct my vision of You. Break off every lie, every distortion. I want to know You as You are—so I can live as I was made. In Jesus' name, Amen.

March 7

*"God is not looking for men with great ability,
but men with great dependability."*
Hudson Taylor

Son,
I'm not impressed by your résumé—
I'm moved by your consistency.

Heaven doesn't need superstars.
It needs sons who show up.
Men who pray when they don't feel it.
Men who love when it's hard.
Men who obey when no one's clapping.

Dependability builds legacy.
Be the man I can trust with the quiet things.
And I'll trust you with the great ones.

"Now it is required that those who have been given a trust must prove faithful." — 1 Corinthians 4:2

Daily Challenge: Pick one habit today that you will show up for every day this month—no matter what.

Warrior's Prayer:
Father, I want to be consistent, not just passionate. Teach me to be faithful in the small things. Make me dependable in Your Kingdom. In Jesus' name, Amen.

March 8

*"God doesn't waste pain. He uses it to
refine, define, and align us."*
Christine Caine

Son,
your pain is not pointless.
Your scars are not wasted.

I use fire
to forge warriors.
I use pressure
to shape purpose.

Every tear
has a testimony.
Every ache
has an assignment.

Don't numb the pain.
Don't run from the ache.

Bring it to Me,
and I'll turn it into something
the enemy never saw coming.

"And we know that in all things God works for the good of those who love Him..." — Romans 8:28

Daily Challenge: Write down one painful moment in your life—and ask God to show you how He's using it for good.

Warrior's Prayer:
Father, I trust You with my pain. I don't want to waste it. Use it to refine me, define me, and align me with Your purpose. In Jesus' name, Amen.

March 9

"We must fear God more than man if we're going to do the work of God among men."
Paul Washer

Son,
you can't please both the crowd and the King.
You'll always serve the one you fear most.

If man's approval rules your heart,
you'll water down truth.
You'll shrink back in battle.
You'll bury the fire.

But if you fear Me—
you'll speak bold.
You'll stand tall.
You'll walk free.

The fear of the Lord is not terror—
it's reverence.
And it's the beginning of real power.

"Fear of man will prove to be a snare, but whoever trusts in the Lord is kept safe." — Proverbs 29:25

Daily Challenge: Speak truth boldly today in one situation where fear would normally keep you silent.

Warrior's Prayer:
Father, burn out fear of man in me. I want to live for Your approval alone. Make me a warrior who trembles at Your Word but never at their opinions. In Jesus' name, Amen.

March 10
"You are the light of the world. Don't hide it—ignite it."
Charles Spurgeon

Son,
you weren't lit to be hidden.
You were born to blaze.

Don't dim your fire
to make others comfortable.
Don't shrink your boldness
to fit the mold.

You are light.
And darkness doesn't negotiate with light—
it flees.

So shine, son.
In every room.
In every space.
Until the shadows can't stay.

"Let your light shine before others, that they may see your good deeds and glorify your Father in heaven." — Matthew 5:16

Daily Challenge: Speak or act in a way today that brings visible light to a dark place—at work, in public, or online.

Warrior's Prayer:
Father, light me up. Let my life burn with the fire of truth, grace, and courage. Teach me to never shrink back. Make me dangerous to darkness. In Jesus' name, Amen.

March 11

*"The prayer that prevails is not the one that
babbles but the one that burns."*
E.M. Bounds

Son,
prayer was never meant to be routine.
It was meant to be warfare.
Fire.
Intimacy.
Authority.

You weren't called to mumble religious words—
you were called to call down Heaven.

Pray like souls are on the line.
Pray like demons listen.
Pray like your family depends on it—
because they do.

Burn on your knees,
and you'll stand like a giant.

"The earnest prayer of a righteous person has great power and produces wonderful results." — James 5:16

Daily Challenge: Set aside 10 minutes today to pray like a warrior—not a routine. Bring passion and purpose.

Warrior's Prayer:
Father, awaken my prayer life. Let fire replace form. Give me boldness, urgency, and hunger when I call on You. Make my words weapons. In Jesus' name, Amen.

March 12

"The Church is looking for better methods.
God is looking for better men."
E.M. Bounds

Son,
I'm not after a platform—
I'm after purity.

The world is obsessed with strategies,
but I'm still searching for men who burn with surrender.

You don't need to be flashy.
You need to be faithful.
Your life is your greatest sermon—
preach it clean.

If I can trust your private life,
I'll anoint your public one.

"The eyes of the Lord search the whole earth in order to strengthen those whose hearts are fully committed to Him." — 2 Chronicles 16:9

Daily Challenge: Do a private heart-check today. Confess anything hidden. Purify the unseen.

Warrior's Prayer:
Father, I want to be a man You can trust. Make me holy in private, not just polished in public. Build me from the inside out. In Jesus' name, Amen.

March 13
"Courage is not the absence of fear, but the mastery of it."
Mark Twain

Son,
courage is not
never feeling afraid.

It is feeling fear—
and choosing to fight anyway.

Cowards run from fear.
Warriors run through it.

You don't need fear to vanish—
you need faith to rise.

Master it.
Name it.
Confront it.
And crush it.

The Spirit in you
is not afraid of anything.

"God has not given us a spirit of fear, but of power and of love and of a sound mind." — 2 Timothy 1:7

Daily Challenge: Identify one fear holding you back—and confront it with action today.

Warrior's Prayer:
Father, I will not be ruled by fear. I refuse to bow to what You've defeated. Fill me with courage, confidence, and clarity. I step into the storm with You beside me. In Jesus' name, Amen.

March 14
"Only one life, 'twill soon be past; only what's done for Christ will last."
C.T. Studd

Son,
your time is limited—
but your impact doesn't have to be.

Every moment spent for Me echoes in eternity.
Every prayer.
Every act of kindness.
Every sacrifice no one saw.

You can't take your possessions with you—
but you can send your purpose ahead.

Don't waste your life chasing what won't last.
Build legacy.
Build eternity.
Build with fire.

"Set your minds on things above, not on earthly things."
— Colossians 3:2

Daily Challenge: Invest in eternity today—disciple, give, serve, or speak. Choose the lasting over the temporary.

Warrior's Prayer:
Father, I want my life to count for more than comfort. Teach me to build with eternity in mind. Help me invest in what cannot be taken away. In Jesus' name, Amen.

March 15

"When obedience ceases to be an irritant and becomes our delight, then God will bless us with power."
Ezra Taft Benson

Son,
I'm not looking for forced compliance—
I'm looking for joyful surrender.

You were never meant to obey Me out of fear—
but out of fierce love.

When obedience becomes your passion,
you unlock a different kind of power.

Not just rule-following.
Not just checkbox Christianity.
But burning allegiance to your King.

I don't bless half-hearted moves.
I bless wholehearted devotion.

"I desire to do Your will, my God; Your law is within my heart." — Psalm 40:8

Daily Challenge: Obey God today in something you've been resisting—and do it with joy.

Warrior's Prayer:
Father, teach me to love obedience. Let surrender become my strength and joy. I don't want to follow reluctantly—I want to follow boldly. In Jesus' name, Amen.

March 16

*"Discipline is the bridge between goals
and accomplishment."*
Jim Rohn

*Son,
desire isn't enough.
Vision without discipline is just a dream.*

*You may want breakthrough.
You may crave victory.
But without daily discipline,
you'll stay stuck in cycles.*

*Discipline is where men are made.
Where warriors are forged.
Where comfort dies
and calling is born.*

*Build your habits,
and your habits will build your legacy.*

"No discipline seems pleasant at the time, but painful. Later on, however, it produces a harvest of righteousness..." — Hebrews 12:11

Daily Challenge: Lock in one area of discipline you've been avoiding—start today. No excuses.

Warrior's Prayer:
Father, build steel in my spirit. Help me train like a son, fight like a soldier, and live like a man of purpose. I choose discipline over excuses. In Jesus' name, Amen.

March 17
"Preach the Gospel at all times. When necessary, use words."
St. Francis of Assisi

Son,
your life is louder than your lips.
People are watching—
not your highlight reel,
but your habits.

When you serve with no credit,
when you forgive when it's hard,
when you stay pure in a filthy world—
you preach with power.

You are My witness in traffic,
at home,
in silence,
and in conflict.

Let your life speak volumes.

"Let your light shine before others, that they may see your good deeds and glorify your Father in heaven." — Matthew 5:16

Daily Challenge: Choose one ordinary moment today to make extraordinary—let your life preach without saying a word.

Warrior's Prayer:
Father, make my life a sermon. Let my actions reflect Your truth. Give me courage to live boldly, even when no one else is watching. In Jesus' name, Amen.

March 18
"Grace is not opposed to effort, it is opposed to earning."
Dallas Willard

Son,
you don't fight for love—
you fight from it.

Grace is not a license to be lazy.
It's fuel for the fire.

You don't earn My favor—
you already have it.

But because you're Mine,
you give everything.
You run hard.
You bleed for the cause.
You fight with joy.

Grace empowers the grind.
It doesn't excuse it.

"But by the grace of God I am what I am... and His grace to me was not without effect." — 1 Corinthians 15:10

Daily Challenge: Reflect today—are you operating from grace or trying to earn it? Shift your mindset and keep pushing.

Warrior's Prayer:
Father, thank You for grace that carries, not just covers. Let me fight with freedom, not fear. Work through me—because I already belong to You. In Jesus' name, Amen.

March 19

"A man is as close to God as he wants to be."
A.W. Tozer

Son,
I've never been far.
The gap between us isn't distance—
it's desire.

You have as much of Me
as you fight for.
As you seek.
As you surrender.

I won't force intimacy—
but I always invite it.

Don't settle for a surface relationship.
Press in.
I reward the relentless.

"Draw near to God, and He will draw near to you."
— James 4:8

Daily Challenge: Spend 15 minutes alone with God today—no music, no agenda, just pursuit.

Warrior's Prayer:
Father, I want more of You. Not just answers, but Your presence. Pull me deeper. Make me hungry for what matters. I will seek until I find. In Jesus' name, Amen.

March 20
"Until you are ready to die, you are not ready to live."
Steven Lawson

Son,
you'll never live fully
until you've settled eternity.

If death still scares you,
you'll play it safe.
You'll protect instead of pursue.
You'll hesitate instead of advance.

But once you've died to yourself,
the enemy loses his grip.

You were born to live free.
And free men are fearless.

> **"For to me, to live is Christ and to die is gain."** — Philippians 1:21

Daily Challenge: Ask yourself: "What would I do differently today if I fully believed death was gain?" Then do it.

Warrior's Prayer:
Father, I surrender the fear of death. Let my life be fearless and free. Make me a man who lives with nothing to lose and everything to gain. In Jesus' name, Amen.

March 21

"You have one business on earth—to save souls."
John Wesley

Son,
your mission is clear:
reach the lost.
That's not optional.
That's not someone else's job.
That's your calling.

I didn't save you so you could sit.
I saved you to send you.

Every room you walk into is an assignment.
Every conversation is an opportunity.

Don't wait for a stage.
Start with your neighbor.
Start with bold love.
Start with truth that sets captives free.

"The fruit of the righteous is a tree of life, and he who wins souls is wise." — Proverbs 11:30

Daily Challenge: Start one spiritual conversation today—plant the seed. Share hope. Don't hesitate.

Warrior's Prayer:
Father, send me today. Open my eyes to see people the way You do. Give me boldness to speak, love to reach, and fire to pursue souls. In Jesus' name, Amen.

March 22

"The world has lost the power to blush over its vice; the Church has lost her power to weep over it."
Leonard Ravenhill

Son,
sin has become normal.
But I didn't call you to be normal.
I called you to be holy.

The world may laugh at darkness,
but you're called to mourn it.
To stand in the gap.
To weep where others wink.

If you want to carry power,
you must carry purity.
Let My holiness break your heart
before you try to change the world.

"Blessed are those who mourn, for they will be comforted." — Matthew 5:4

Daily Challenge: Spend time today in honest repentance—not for guilt, but to realign with God's holiness.

Warrior's Prayer:
Father, break my heart for what breaks Yours. Let me not become numb to sin. Fill me with holy fire that burns away compromise. I want to carry Your heart. In Jesus' name, Amen.

March 23
"The Christian life is not a playground—it's a battleground."
Warren Wiersbe

Son,
this isn't a game.
It's a war.

You weren't saved to stay safe.
You were born again to battle.

No more spectators.
No more sidelines.

Arm up.
Pray hard.
Speak truth.
Lead well.

There's a real enemy,
and real souls on the line.

Don't play church.
Be the Church.

"Put on the full armor of God, so that you can take your stand against the devil's schemes." — Ephesians 6:11

Daily Challenge: Identify one area where you've been passive in the battle—and take action today.

Warrior's Prayer:
Father, I was not saved to sit. Train my hands for war. Show me where to stand and how to fight. Let me live every day like souls depend on it—because they do. In Jesus' name, Amen.

March 24

"You never have to recover from a genuine move of God."
Lou Engle

Son,
when I move,
everything changes.
Your heart.
Your habits.
Your fire.

You weren't created for casual Christianity.
You were made for encounter.
Real. Raw.
Life-altering.

Don't settle for moments.
Seek movements.
Stay hungry for more.
Because I never stop pouring—
when you never stop pursuing.

"Blessed are those who hunger and thirst for righteousness, for they will be filled." — Matthew 5:6

Daily Challenge: Ask God for a fresh encounter today—and position yourself to receive it with hunger.

Warrior's Prayer:
Father, I don't want routine—I want You. Stir up a hunger in me that never fades. Fill me with fresh fire. Let revival start in my soul today. In Jesus' name, Amen.

March 25

"When the devil sees a man or woman who really believes in prayer, he trembles as much as he ever did."
R.A. Torrey

Son,
prayer isn't passive.
It's power.
It shifts atmospheres.
It stops hell in its tracks.

When you pray with authority,
you strike where swords can't.
You reach what hands can't.
You change what people think can't be changed.

Don't pray safe—
pray dangerous.
Pray like you've already won.
Because in Me, you have.

"The weapons we fight with are not the weapons of the world... they have divine power to demolish strongholds." — 2 Corinthians 10:4

Daily Challenge: Pray boldly today for something that feels impossible. Aim high. Ask hard.

Warrior's Prayer:
Father, teach me to pray with fire. To intercede with authority. To believe for the impossible. Let my prayers shake the ground and bring Heaven down. In Jesus' name, Amen.

March 26

"A single day in the presence of God is better than a thousand spent in human glory."
David Brainerd

Son,
the spotlight can never heal your soul.
Applause will never satisfy your spirit.
But one moment with Me
can transform everything.

Don't chase platforms—
pursue presence.

You weren't made to be famous—
you were made to be filled.
The greatest victories of your life
will be won in the quiet place.

Live from My presence,
not for their praise.

"Better is one day in Your courts than a thousand elsewhere..." — Psalm 84:10

Daily Challenge: Spend quality time alone with God today before giving yourself to anything else.

Warrior's Prayer:
Father, I choose You over everything else. Silence the noise around me. Let Your presence fill me, define me, and lead me. I don't want a moment without You. In Jesus' name, Amen.

March 27

*"Holiness is not the way to Christ. Christ is
the way to holiness."*
Adrian Rogers

Son,
you don't work your way to Me.
You walk with Me,
and I work My holiness into you.

Stop trying to be clean enough
to approach Me.
You were never meant to fix yourself—
you were meant to follow Me.

Holiness isn't perfection—
it's proximity.

Stay close to Me,
and sin will lose its grip.

"But just as He who called you is holy, so be holy in all you do." — 1 Peter 1:15

Daily Challenge: Don't perform for God—pursue Him. Draw near, and let holiness grow from the inside out.

Warrior's Prayer:
Father, thank You that holiness isn't earned—it's imparted through walking with You. Keep me close. Change me from the inside out. In Jesus' name, Amen.

March 28

"If you don't have a sword, sell your cloak and buy one."
Jesus (Luke 22:36)

Son,
this is not peacetime.
This is war.

The sword is not just Scripture—
it's your readiness.
Your training.
Your resolve.

No more soft faith.
No more excuses.
No more waiting for a safer time.

Arm up.
Gear up.
Show up.

Because the enemy
doesn't care about your comfort—
he fears your courage.

"Be strong in the Lord and in His mighty power. Put on the full armor of God..." — Ephesians 6:10–11

Daily Challenge: Do something today that sharpens your edge—spiritually or physically. Get back in the fight.

Warrior's Prayer:
Father, I will not live soft. Equip me. Train me. Make me a weapon in Your hand. Let me never forget the war I was born into. In Jesus' name, Amen.

March 29
"You are not fighting for victory—you are fighting from it."
Tony Evans

Son,
the war has already been won.
The tomb is empty.
The throne is occupied.
The enemy is defeated.

You don't fight hoping to win—
you fight knowing I already have.

Stand in victory.
Speak from authority.
Live like a man who knows the outcome.

Because the blood still speaks,
and My Spirit still empowers.

"But thanks be to God! He gives us the victory through our Lord Jesus Christ." — 1 Corinthians 15:57

Daily Challenge: In every challenge today, declare: "I'm not fighting for victory—I'm fighting from it."

Warrior's Prayer:
Father, remind me today that I am not alone, not weak, and not losing. I stand in the victory of Jesus Christ. Let me fight with faith, not fear. In Jesus' name, Amen.

March 30
"If you want to lead men, learn to weep before God."
Leonard Ravenhill

Son,
real leadership doesn't start with strength—
it starts with surrender.

You don't become a great man
by dominating people—
you become one
by interceding for them.

Weep before Me
so you can stand before them.
Bring their names to Me
before you speak a word to them.

Leaders bleed in secret
so they can lead in public.

"Let your priests be clothed with righteousness, and let Your saints shout for joy." — Psalm 132:9

Daily Challenge: Pray for someone you lead today with deep sincerity. Intercede, don't just instruct.

Warrior's Prayer:
Father, give me a heart that weeps before You for the people I lead. Break me for what burdens them. Teach me to lead from the secret place. In Jesus' name, Amen.

March 31
"It is a poor soldier who is not always ready to fight."
Martin Luther

Son,
you don't get to pick when the battle comes.
You only get to choose if you'll be ready.

This isn't a weekend war.
This is every day,
every decision,
every thought.

Your mind is a battlefield.
Your family is under fire.
Your habits are either weapons or weaknesses.

Stay ready.
Live alert.
Keep the sword sharp and your knees bent.

"Be alert and of sober mind. Your enemy the devil prowls around like a roaring lion..." — 1 Peter 5:8

Daily Challenge: Evaluate your current condition. Are you battle-ready? If not, fix it today.

Warrior's Prayer:
Father, keep me sharp. Make me alert to the real war around me. I will not be caught off guard. Prepare my hands for battle and my heart for obedience. In Jesus' name, Amen.

April 1

"God is not looking for extraordinary people. He's looking for ordinary people who will trust an extraordinary God."
J. Hudson Taylor

Son,
you don't need to be spectacular—
you just need to be surrendered.

You were never called to impress the world.
You were called to obey Me.
Simple faith.
Daily trust.
Radical availability.

I do extraordinary things
through ordinary men
who simply say "yes."

If you're waiting to feel ready—stop.
Just move.
I'll fill the gap.

"We have this treasure in jars of clay to show that this all-surpassing power is from God and not from us."
— 2 Corinthians 4:7

Daily Challenge: Say "yes" to God today before you have all the answers. Step. Trust. Go.

Warrior's Prayer:
Father, I'm done waiting to feel qualified. Use me right here, right now. I may be ordinary—but I serve an extraordinary God. I say yes. In Jesus' name, Amen.

April 2

"Don't shine so others can see you. Shine so that through you, others can see Him."
C.S. Lewis

Son,
this life isn't about your brand—
it's about My glory.

You weren't created to draw attention to yourself.
You were created to reflect Me.

Let your strength point to My grace.
Let your courage point to My Spirit.
Let your victory point to My cross.

The world doesn't need a celebrity—
it needs a mirror.
Shine bright.
And let them see Me through you.

"For we do not preach ourselves, but Jesus Christ as Lord..." — 2 Corinthians 4:5

Daily Challenge: In one moment of praise or recognition today—deflect the glory to God. Publicly or privately.

Warrior's Prayer:
Father, when people see my life, let them see You. I don't want to be impressive—I want to be a reflection. Shine through me in every word, every win, and every battle. In Jesus' name, Amen.

April 3

"The man who kneels before God can stand before anyone."
Leonard Ravenhill

Son,
courage is not found
in crowds,
but in closets.

You don't need applause
to stand.
You need intimacy.

You won't find boldness
in the gym,
or the mirror—
you'll find it
on your knees.

Kneel often.
Kneel deep.
Kneel with tears.

Then rise
with fire.

"But when you pray, go into your room, close the door and pray to your Father, who is unseen..."
— Matthew 6:6

Daily Challenge: Go to your knees today—literally—and pray in private. No rush. Just you and God.

Warrior's Prayer:
Father, I kneel before You so I can rise with courage. Burn in me during the quiet so I can roar in the open. I don't want stage power—I want secret place fire. In Jesus' name, Amen.

April 4
"If you're not dead, God's not done."
Craig Groeschel

Son,
if you're still breathing,
you're still in the fight.

Don't you dare count yourself out.
Don't you quit because you feel tired.
I've still got purpose in your bones,
power in your breath,
and assignments for your hands.

Scars don't disqualify you—
they prepare you.
Delay doesn't mean denial.
This isn't over.

Rise up.
You've got ground to take.

"Being confident of this, that He who began a good work in you will carry it on to completion..." — Philippians 1:6

Daily Challenge: Encourage someone (including yourself) who feels like giving up. Speak life over unfinished purpose.

Warrior's Prayer:
Father, thank You for not being done with me. Breathe new strength into my lungs. Restore my passion, reignite my mission, and raise me up for the next battle. In Jesus' name, Amen.

April 5

"God does not call those who are equipped, He equips those whom He calls."
Smith Wigglesworth

Son,
your calling isn't based on your résumé—
it's based on My voice.

If I've called you,
I will equip you.
If I've assigned you,
I will sustain you.

Don't shrink back because of what you lack.
I specialize in using the unqualified.
I get the glory when you walk
in what only I can supply.

Step forward in faith.
I'll meet you with fire.

"The one who calls you is faithful, and He will do it."
— 1 Thessalonians 5:24

Daily Challenge: Act boldly today in an area you feel unqualified—and trust God to meet you there.

Warrior's Prayer:
Father, You've called me—and that's enough. Equip me for everything You've assigned me. I step forward with courage, knowing You will do what I can't. In Jesus' name, Amen.

April 6

"To be a Christian means to forgive the inexcusable because God has forgiven the inexcusable in you."
C.S. Lewis

Son,
forgiveness isn't weakness—
it's war.

It breaks the chains the enemy wants to keep wrapped around your soul.
Bitterness is bondage.
But forgiveness?
It's freedom.

You forgive not because they deserve it—
but because I forgave you first.
Let it go.
Not for them—
but for your freedom, your calling, your fire.

Real warriors don't carry grudges—
they drop them and carry the cross instead.

"Forgive as the Lord forgave you." — Colossians 3:13

Daily Challenge: Forgive someone today—out loud, in prayer, or in person. Release it for good.

Warrior's Prayer:
Father, I release the weight. I forgive what I've held on to. Not because they earned it, but because You gave it to me first. Free my heart to move forward. In Jesus' name, Amen.

April 7

"The measure of a man's greatness is not the number of servants he has, but the number of people he serves."
John Hagee

Son,
My Kingdom isn't about climbing—
it's about kneeling.

If you want to lead,
serve.
If you want to be great,
get lower.

The world celebrates power,
but I celebrate sacrifice.

Start with the towel,
not the title.
Lay your life down—
that's where legacy begins.

"Whoever wants to become great among you must be your servant." — Matthew 20:26

Daily Challenge: Serve someone today with no credit, no spotlight, and no agenda. Do it in secret.

Warrior's Prayer:
Father, teach me to lead like Jesus—with a towel in my hand and love in my heart. Let greatness in Your Kingdom look like service through mine. In Jesus' name, Amen.

April 8

"You can't defeat the enemy if you're still entertaining him."
John Ramirez

Son,
you can't conquer
what you still cuddle.

You can't slay the serpent
you secretly feed.

Stop flirting with what
I've called you to kill.

Don't excuse it.
Don't manage it.
Don't hide it behind a mask of "grace."

Expose it.
End it.
Evict it.

You weren't called
to coexist with the enemy—
you were called to crush him.

"Do not give the devil a foothold." — *Ephesians 4:27*

Daily Challenge: Identify one sin or temptation you've justified—repent, confess it, and shut the door.

Warrior's Prayer:
Father, show me where I've entertained the enemy. Give me holy anger and the courage to slam the door shut. I don't want to manage sin—I want to kill it. In Jesus' name, Amen.

April 9

"God never said the weapons wouldn't form. He said they wouldn't prosper."
T.D. Jakes

Son,
the attack is real—
but so is your armor.

I never promised comfort.
I promised victory.
So when the weapon forms,
don't panic—prepare.

Raise your shield.
Stand your ground.
Worship while you wait.
Warriors aren't surprised by warfare.

The enemy may strike—
but My promise still stands.

"No weapon forged against you will prevail..." — Isaiah 54:17

Daily Challenge: Face one battle today with confidence. Declare: "It may form, but it won't win."

Warrior's Prayer:
Father, I won't fear the attack—I'll trust the outcome. Your Word is my defense. I declare today that no weapon formed against me will prosper. In Jesus' name, Amen.

April 10

*"When you get to the end of yourself, you find
the beginning of God."*
Billy Graham

*Son,
your strength has limits—
Mine doesn't.*

*I'm not asking you to be enough.
I'm asking you to surrender.
Because when your strength runs out,
My power starts to rise.*

*You don't have to fake it.
You don't have to push harder.
You have to let go.*

*Lay it down,
and watch Me do what only I can.*

"But He said to me, 'My grace is sufficient for you, for My power is made perfect in weakness.'"
— 2 Corinthians 12:9

Daily Challenge: Identify one area where you're exhausted. Stop striving. Surrender it to God today.

Warrior's Prayer:
Father, I reach the end of me—and I find You waiting. Take what I can't carry. I surrender the pressure and pick up Your peace. Your grace is enough. In Jesus' name, Amen.

April 11
*"The will of God will never take you where the
grace of God cannot sustain you."*
Billy Graham

Son,
I never send you into battle alone.
I never assign you to a mission without supplying strength.

You may not feel ready—
but I am.
You may not see the way—
but I do.

Grace isn't just what saves you—
it's what carries you.
It's the wind behind your obedience
and the strength beneath your surrender.

Where I lead, I sustain.
Where I call, I provide.

"My grace is sufficient for you, for My power is made perfect in weakness." — 2 Corinthians 12:9

Daily Challenge: Step boldly into something you've delayed—trust God's grace to sustain your obedience.

Warrior's Prayer:
Father, I will go where You lead because I trust You to carry me. I won't wait until I feel ready—if You called me, You will keep me. Strengthen me with grace today. In Jesus' name, Amen.

April 12

"You cannot correct what you are unwilling to confront."
Craig Groeschel

Son,
ignoring the issue won't fix it.
Avoiding the conversation won't heal it.
You're not called to comfort—
you're called to courage.

Confrontation isn't anger—
it's love in action.
It's clarity with conviction.
It's stepping into the tension
instead of tiptoeing around it.

I didn't put fear in you—
I put truth and boldness in your bones.

So speak.
Move.
Lead.

"Speak the truth in love..." — Ephesians 4:15

Daily Challenge: Confront one situation today that you've been avoiding. Do it with truth and love.

Warrior's Prayer:
Father, help me lead with courage. I don't want to stay silent when You've called me to speak. Teach me to confront with wisdom and truth. In Jesus' name, Amen.

April 13

"He is no fool who gives what he cannot keep to gain what he cannot lose."
Jim Elliot

Son,
this world is loud,
but it's not lasting.

You can't keep the car.
The title.
The applause.
The status.

But you can gain something eternal.
Something holy.
Something that doesn't rust or rot.

Lay it down.
Let it go.
Give it up.

Because what you surrender now
turns into a reward
that no one can steal.

"Store up for yourselves treasures in heaven..."
— Matthew 6:20

Daily Challenge: Let go of something temporary today to invest in something eternal—time, attention, resources, or pride.

Warrior's Prayer:
Father, teach me to live for what lasts. I surrender anything that steals my focus from You. Let my life be an investment in eternity. In Jesus' name, Amen.

April 14
"If God is your partner, make your plans big."
D.L. Moody

Son,
stop playing small.
Stop praying like you serve a weak God.

I didn't call you to survive—
I called you to shake the gates of hell.
Dream bigger.
Pray harder.
Move boldly.

If I'm with you,
there are no limits.
If I'm in it,
you can't fail.

Kingdom warriors think beyond comfort zones.
They walk in Kingdom size faith.

"Now to Him who is able to do immeasurably more than all we ask or imagine..." — Ephesians 3:20

Daily Challenge: Write down the biggest prayer you've been afraid to pray—then pray it out loud with faith.

Warrior's Prayer:
Father, forgive me for playing small. You are the God of the impossible. Stretch my faith. Ignite my imagination. Let me dream in proportion to Your power. In Jesus' name, Amen.

April 15

*"Temptation is the devil looking through the keyhole.
Yielding is opening the door and inviting him in."*
Billy Sunday

*Son,
temptation is not sin—
but it is a signal.*

*It tells you the enemy sees your potential.
That you're too dangerous to leave alone.*

*But the choice is still yours:
Open the door, or shut it.
Entertain the thought, or end it.
Flirt with fire, or walk away in power.*

*You're not powerless.
You're not outnumbered.
You've got the Spirit of God inside you—
act like it.*

"Submit yourselves, then, to God. Resist the devil, and he will flee from you." — James 4:7

Daily Challenge: Recognize one area of temptation and actively shut the door—physically, digitally, or mentally.

Warrior's Prayer:
Father, I won't let the enemy linger. Expose the trap, and give me the strength to resist. I choose obedience over indulgence. I slam the door on temptation today. In Jesus' name, Amen.

April 16
"You may choose to look the other way, but you can never say again that you did not know."
William Wilberforce

Son,
once your eyes are opened,
you carry responsibility.

You weren't saved to stay safe—
you were saved to stand in the gap.
For the trafficked.
For the fatherless.
For the silent suffering in your community.

You are light.
And light doesn't look away.
It steps forward,
into darkness,
with truth and compassion.

"Rescue those being led away to death; hold back those staggering toward slaughter." — Proverbs 24:11

Daily Challenge: Research a cause that breaks your heart—pray, give, or take one bold step to get involved.

Warrior's Prayer:
Father, don't let me look away. Open my eyes and break my heart for what breaks Yours. Show me where to step in and how to lead with love and truth. In Jesus' name, Amen.

April 17
"The mark of a great man is not how he handles success, but how he handles failure."
T.W. Hunt

Son,
your failures don't define you—
but how you respond to them does.

Do you run?
Hide?
Blame?
Or do you stand up, face it, and learn?

I don't use perfect men.
I use redeemed men.
Men who fall,
but refuse to stay down.

Failure isn't the end—
it's the training ground for greatness.

"Though the righteous fall seven times, they rise again..."
— Proverbs 24:16

Daily Challenge: Reflect on a past failure. Write down what it taught you—and how it can strengthen others.

Warrior's Prayer:
Father, I won't hide from my failures—I'll grow from them. Redeem every mistake and turn it into a lesson. Let my scars preach of Your grace. In Jesus' name, Amen.

April 18
"There are no shortcuts to any place worth going."
Beverly Sills

Son,
you can't microwave maturity.
You can't shortcut sanctification.

The long road
is the holy road.
The narrow path
is the warrior's way.

Stay faithful.
Stay gritty.
Stay focused
when no one's clapping.

There's glory
in the grind.
There's strength
in the slow burn.

Endure the process—
and I'll build a legacy in you.

"Let perseverance finish its work so that you may be mature and complete, not lacking anything."
— James 1:4

Daily Challenge: Identify one area you've been rushing—slow down and recommit to the process.

Warrior's Prayer:
Father, I surrender my timeline. Forge me through the process. Make me strong through the slow. Teach me to embrace the long road with joy. In Jesus' name, Amen.

April 19

"A Bible that's falling apart usually belongs to someone who isn't."
Charles Spurgeon

Son,
this world will shake you—
but My Word will anchor you.

It's not decoration.
It's your weapon.
Your compass.
Your lifeline in the war.

Don't wait for the storm to learn how to wield it.
Train now.
Consume truth.
Let it renew your mind
and ignite your courage.

"Your word is a lamp to my feet and a light to my path."
— Psalm 119:105

Daily Challenge: Spend 20 minutes in the Word today. Don't skim—dig deep. Let it speak, challenge, and strengthen you.

Warrior's Prayer:
Father, make me a man of the Word. Let Scripture take root in me so deep that I cannot be shaken. Light my path. Fill my heart. Train my hands. In Jesus' name, Amen.

April 20
"To be filled with the Spirit is to be filled with the life of Christ Himself."
Andrew Murray

Son,
you weren't called to live for Me in your strength—
you were called to live through Me in Mine.

The Holy Spirit isn't just a helper—
He's your power source.
Your fire.
Your wisdom in the fight.

Stop relying on discipline alone.
Start walking in daily dependence.
My Spirit doesn't visit—
He dwells,
He equips,
He overflows.

Let Me fill you fresh today.

"Be filled with the Spirit." — Ephesians 5:18

Daily Challenge: Before anything else today, ask to be freshly filled with the Holy Spirit—and walk in awareness of His presence.

Warrior's Prayer:
Holy Spirit, fill me again. Take every corner of my heart. Empower me to walk like Jesus walked. Let Your presence be my power in every step. In Jesus' name, Amen.

April 21
"If you're not ready to die for it, take the word 'faith' out of your vocabulary."
Vance Havner

Son,
this isn't feel-good faith—
this is die-to-live,
lose-to-win,
risk-it-all-for-the-King faith.

Faith that doesn't cost you anything
isn't faith—
it's fiction.

I'm not looking for safe men.
I'm looking for surrendered ones.
Warriors who don't just speak truth,
but bleed for it.

You don't have to die daily
because it's easy.
You die daily
because it's holy.

"Whoever wants to be My disciple must deny themselves and take up their cross daily and follow Me."
— Luke 9:23

Daily Challenge: Identify one area where you've played it safe—lay it down, pick up your cross, and move boldly.

Warrior's Prayer:
Father, I'm not here to play it safe—I'm here to walk in surrender. Let me die daily to comfort, pride, and fear. Make me bold, battle-ready, and fully Yours. In Jesus' name, Amen.

April 22
"When Christ calls a man, He bids him come and die."
Dietrich Bonhoeffer

Son,
discipleship isn't a brand—
it's a bloodline.

I didn't call you to ease.
I called you to war.
To die to yourself,
to your ego,
to your plans.

That death is the doorway to life.
To power.
To freedom.
To a legacy that makes hell tremble.

So don't sugarcoat the cost.
Carry it with joy.
Because resurrection always follows the grave.

"I have been crucified with Christ and I no longer live, but Christ lives in me." — Galatians 2:20

Daily Challenge: Fast from something today that feeds the flesh—die to it with purpose.

Warrior's Prayer:
Father, kill what's in me that keeps me from You. Let my life echo the death and resurrection of Jesus. I choose the narrow road, no matter the cost. In Jesus' name, Amen.

April 23

*"Live in such a way that if someone spoke badly of you,
no one would believe it."*
Charles Spurgeon

*Son,
your integrity
is your armor.*

*Not perfection—
but consistency.
Private obedience.
Invisible strength.*

*It's what you do
when no one is looking
that makes you dangerous
when everyone is.*

*Let your life be so clean
that slander slides off like oil.
Let your habits
preach louder than your words.*

*Live so holy
you leave no room for doubt.*

"In everything set them an example by doing what is good. In your teaching show integrity..." — Titus 2:7

Daily Challenge: Audit your hidden habits. Strengthen one area today where integrity has slipped.

Warrior's Prayer:
Father, make me a man of truth from the inside out. May my private life please You more than my public image. Build in me unshakable integrity. In Jesus' name, Amen.

April 24

*"The greatest tragedy in life is not death,
but a life without purpose."*
Myles Munroe

*Son,
don't mistake movement for mission.
Busyness for calling.
Success for obedience.*

*You weren't put here to just get by.
You were born with purpose written in your DNA.
There's fire in your bones,
legacy in your blood,
and glory in your obedience.*

*So stop chasing what won't last.
Seek what matters most.
Find your purpose—
and give it everything you've got.*

"Before I formed you in the womb I knew you, before you were born I set you apart..." — Jeremiah 1:5

Daily Challenge: Write down your God-given mission in one sentence—and align one action today with it.

Warrior's Prayer:
Father, reveal and refine my purpose. Strip away distractions and focus my heart on what You made me for. Let me live full out, no regrets. In Jesus' name, Amen.

April 25

"Don't pray for tasks equal to your power. Pray for power equal to your tasks."
Phillips Brooks

Son,
you weren't meant to rely on your strength—
you were meant to draw from Mine.

If the vision overwhelms you,
you're probably hearing Me right.
I don't call you to what's comfortable.
I call you to what's impossible—
so you'll stay close.

You don't need more talent.
You need more trust.
More dependence.
More fire from above.

"Not by might nor by power, but by My Spirit, says the Lord Almighty." — Zechariah 4:6

Daily Challenge: Face one hard task today with supernatural prayer instead of natural strength.

Warrior's Prayer:
Father, I ask for power beyond my limits. Fill me with Your Spirit to do what I can't in my own strength. Let my life show the world what You can do through a surrendered man. In Jesus' name, Amen.

April 26
"God writes straight with crooked lines."
Spanish Proverb

Son,
what you see as a mistake,
I see as a masterpiece in progress.

You think it's chaos—
I know it's construction.
You think you're off course—
I know you're right on schedule.

Every scar is a sentence.
Every fall is a forge.
Every tear is a tool in My hand.

You are not lost.
You are being led.
Trust Me to make beauty from the broken.

"Being confident of this, that He who began a good work in you will carry it on to completion..." — Philippians 1:6

Daily Challenge: Thank God today for one "crooked line" in your life—a scar, a failure, a broken chapter He's redeeming.

Warrior's Prayer:
Father, I trust the Author of my story. Even when the lines look crooked to me, I know You are writing a masterpiece. Finish what You started in me. In Jesus' name, Amen.

April 27

*"The man who walks with God always
reaches his destination."*
Corrie ten Boom

*Son,
you don't have to have it all figured out—
you just have to stay close to Me.*

*Success isn't about speed—
it's about steps of faith.*

*Detours don't derail My plan.
Delays don't deny your destiny.*

*Every step with Me
is a step toward purpose,
even when it feels hidden.*

*Just keep walking, son.
I'll get you exactly where you're meant to be.*

"In all your ways acknowledge Him, and He will make your paths straight." — Proverbs 3:6

Daily Challenge: Walk physically or spiritually today in silence with God—invite Him to direct your steps.

Warrior's Prayer:
Father, I won't rush. I won't panic. I will walk with You step by step, knowing You are shaping the road ahead. I trust You with the journey. In Jesus' name, Amen.

April 28
"Courage is fear that has said its prayers."
Karl Barth

Son,
courage isn't
the absence of fear.
It's the refusal to let fear rule.

Fear will shout.
Fear will threaten.

But when you pray,
fear loses its teeth.

When you kneel,
courage stands.

You don't need more bravery.
You need deeper surrender.

Because the man who prays
walks fearless into the fire.

"Be strong and courageous. Do not be afraid... for the Lord your God goes with you." — Deuteronomy 31:6

Daily Challenge: Pray before you face any fear today—don't act first, pray first.

Warrior's Prayer:
Father, when fear rises, I choose to kneel first. Give me the courage that comes from Your Spirit. Help me walk boldly into everything You've called me to. In Jesus' name, Amen.

April 29
*"The greatest enemy of faith may be not
fear—but forgetfulness."*
John Piper

Son,
don't forget what I've already done.
Don't forget the battles I already won.
Don't forget the mountains I already moved.

Fear feeds on forgetfulness—
but faith feeds on remembrance.

Remember My faithfulness yesterday,
and you'll have fire for today.

Stack your victories.
Remember the moments I came through.
Replay My goodness in your mind
until fear has no place left to hide.

"I will remember the deeds of the Lord; yes, I will remember Your miracles of long ago." — Psalm 77:11

Daily Challenge: Write down three moments God came through for you—and thank Him specifically for each one.

Warrior's Prayer:
Father, I remember. I will not forget Your faithfulness. When fear whispers lies, I will shout testimonies. Thank You for every victory behind me and every promise ahead. In Jesus' name, Amen.

April 30

*"All that I am I owe to Jesus Christ, revealed
to me in His divine Book."*
David Livingstone

Son,
everything you are,
everything you will ever be,
is rooted in Me.

Your strength is borrowed.
Your breath is gifted.
Your purpose is assigned.

You don't have to manufacture greatness—
you just have to remain in Me.

Anchor your life in My Word.
Bury your dreams in My soil.
Drink deeply from My Spirit.

And I will grow in you a life
that hell itself can't uproot.

"I am the vine; you are the branches. If you remain in Me and I in you, you will bear much fruit..." — John 15:5

Daily Challenge: Recommit today to being rooted in God's Word—set a new standard for daily immersion.

Warrior's Prayer:
Father, I owe it all to You. Without You, I am nothing—through You, I can bear much fruit. Root me deep in Your Word, Your presence, and Your Spirit. Make my life unshakable in You. In Jesus' name, Amen.

May 1
*"God will not protect you from what He
will perfect you through."*
Lisa Bevere

Son,
I see the fire you're walking through. I know it feels fierce, and the heat is real. But listen to Me: I'm not using this fire to destroy you—I'm using it to define you. Every trial is a tool in My hands, shaping a warrior who cannot be broken. I'm not protecting you from the fire because I am perfecting you through it.

You were not made for comfort. You were made for conquest. I have placed a steel inside your soul that can only be revealed through resistance. Don't fear the flames—fear walking away from the work I'm doing inside of you. Trust My hands even when you can't trace My plan. I am refining you for victories you cannot yet see.

You are not being punished. You are being prepared.

"When you walk through the fire, you will not be burned; the flames will not set you ablaze." — Isaiah 43:2

Daily Challenge: Today, embrace one uncomfortable thing without complaining. See it as God's fire forging you stronger, not as an attack.

Warrior's Prayer:
Father, when the fire comes, remind me You are still with me. Strengthen my heart to trust Your refining hand. I don't want to waste the wilderness or the fire. Use every trial to shape me into the warrior You designed. I will not fear the flames. I will follow You through them. In Jesus' name, Amen.

May 2

*"The will of God will never take you where the
grace of God cannot sustain you."*
Billy Graham

Son,

you fear the unknown because you forget Who's already there. I don't send you into battles I haven't already prepared you to win. You will face storms, yes—but not alone. My grace is not distant. It is the very oxygen you breathe in the battlefield.

When the mountain looks too high, My grace lifts you. When the valley looks too dark, My grace lights your way. You don't have to muscle your way through this season—you have to trust My strength more than your own. Walk forward boldly. My grace goes before you, surrounds you, and follows behind you. You are carried even when you think you're crawling.

My grace is enough, son. It always has been. It always will be.

"My grace is sufficient for you, for My power is made perfect in weakness." — 2 Corinthians 12:9

Daily Challenge: Whenever you feel overwhelmed today, pause and say out loud, "Your grace is enough for me." Walk forward in that confidence.

Warrior's Prayer:
Father, thank You for the grace that covers every step, every fall, and every fight. Teach me to lean on You and not my own strength. Your grace is my banner and my battle cry. I move forward today, not because I am strong, but because You are. In Jesus' name, Amen.

May 3

"Out of suffering have emerged the strongest souls; the most massive characters are seared with scars."
Kahlil Gibran

Son,
you carry scars like shame.
I see them as songs.
You flinch at your wounds.
I weave them into weapons.
You try to hide your limp.
I teach you to lead with it.

The ones who limp with Me
march stronger than those who sprint without Me.
The scarred ones know the sound of real victory.
Not the clean, polished kind—
but the bloody, hard-won kind
that terrifies hell itself.

Wear your scars like armor, son.
They are proof you fought,
proof you stayed,
proof you belong to Me.

"But He said to me, 'My grace is sufficient for you, for My power is made perfect in weakness.' Therefore I will boast all the more gladly about my weaknesses, so that Christ's power may rest on me." — 2 Corinthians 12:9

Daily Challenge: Write down one scar in your life—and next to it, write how God used (or is using) it to build you stronger.

Warrior's Prayer:
Father, thank You for scars that tell stories of survival and redemption. I will no longer hide them. I will wear them as testimony to Your strength in my weakness. Teach me to lead with my limp and glorify You in every wound. In Jesus' name, Amen.

May 4

"Faith is not the belief that God will do what you want. It is the belief that God will do what is right."
Max Lucado

Son,
stop measuring My faithfulness by your feelings. I am good even when the story feels bad. I am just even when the journey feels unfair. I am right even when the road feels wrong. Faith isn't trusting that you'll always understand—it's trusting that I always reign.

Sometimes you'll pray for rescue—and I'll answer by building your resilience. Sometimes you'll cry for escape—and I'll strengthen you to endure. Trust isn't a tool to get your way; it's a weapon to stay My way. You are being shaped for higher battles, and the hammering is holy. Stay anchored, son. I am doing what is right, even when it doesn't feel easy.

"Trust in the Lord with all your heart and lean not on your own understanding." — Proverbs 3:5

Daily Challenge: Choose to trust God today in one situation you don't understand. Say, "God, I trust You to do what's right."

Warrior's Prayer:
Father, strengthen my trust when my understanding fails. You are good. You are right. You are faithful. I surrender my need to control or explain. Lead me, shape me, and use me for Your glory. In Jesus' name, Amen.

May 5

*"Your potential is the sum of all the possibilities
God has for your life."*
Charles Stanley

Son,
you are not called to live safe—you are called to live sent.
You are not called to stay comfortable—you are called to
conquer. The potential I placed in you is not small, fragile,
or ordinary. It is explosive, eternal, and world-shaking when
unleashed in obedience.

You haven't seen even a fraction of what I can do through
you when you surrender fully. Stop playing small. Stop
shrinking back. The world doesn't need another polished
imitation—it needs a blazing original, filled with My Spirit,
walking in raw, reckless obedience. That's you, son. Rise up.
Step out. Dare greatly for My Kingdom.

"Now to Him who is able to do immeasurably more than all we ask or imagine, according to His power that is at work within us." — Ephesians 3:20

Daily Challenge: Take one bold step today toward something you've been hesitating to do for God. Even if it's small—move.

Warrior's Prayer:
Father, awaken the full potential You placed inside me. I refuse to live small. Ignite a holy fire in my soul to walk in bold obedience and fierce faith. Use me in ways bigger than I can imagine. In Jesus' name, Amen.

May 6

"We are all pencils in the hand of a writing God who is sending love letters to the world."
Mother Teresa

Son,
you want to be the sword.
I made you the pen.
You want to conquer kingdoms.
I called you to change hearts.
You want to shout.
I called you to serve.

A warrior's strength
isn't measured by his noise,
but by his nearness to Me.

Let Me write through you.
Let Me bleed grace through your pages.
You don't have to craft the story—
you just have to stay in My hand.

You are My letter to a broken world, son.
Let Me write love in every area through you.

"You yourselves are our letter, written on our hearts, known and read by everyone." — 2 Corinthians 3:2

Daily Challenge: Serve one person today quietly and intentionally—no announcement, no recognition. Just love.

Warrior's Prayer:
Father, I surrender my life to be Your pen. Write Your love through my actions and my attitude. Let my life be a living letter of grace to those around me. Make my story Your masterpiece. In Jesus' name, Amen.

May 7
"Worry does not empty tomorrow of its sorrow;
it empties today of its strength."
Corrie ten Boom

Son,

worry is a thief, and it steals what I have given you for today. When you live tangled in fears about the future, you miss the strength I am providing in the present. I have not called you to carry tomorrow's burdens with today's grace.

You are not designed to live two days at once. Walk with Me in this moment. Trust Me with this step. Fear will always project shadows larger than reality—but My truth stands brighter and stronger than any fear. Fix your eyes on Me, not the what-ifs. I already hold your tomorrows in My hands. Your strength is here. Your victory is here. Your peace is here—now.

"Therefore do not worry about tomorrow, for tomorrow will worry about itself. Each day has enough trouble of its own." — Matthew 6:34

Daily Challenge: Every time you catch yourself worrying today, stop and pray: "Father, I trust You with this."

Warrior's Prayer:
Father, forgive me for the times I let worry steal my strength. Today, I choose to trust You moment by moment. You are my security, my provider, and my protector. I will not fear the future, because You are already there. In Jesus' name, Amen.

May 8

*"Never be afraid to trust an unknown future
to a known God."*
Corrie ten Boom

Son,
you are chasing answers.
I am teaching you to chase Me.
You are reaching for certainty.
I am reaching for your heart.

Faith is not seeing the map.
Faith is taking My hand
and walking blind
with trust burning brighter than fear.

Every step you take with Me,
even when you can't see,
echoes in eternity.
Your obedience is the victory.
Not the outcome.
Not the arrival.
The obedience.

Let's walk, son.
Step by step.
Hand in hand.
Heart in heart.

"For we walk by faith, not by sight." — 2 Corinthians 5:7

Daily Challenge: Take one step today that requires faith instead of certainty. Move forward even if you can't see all the details.

Warrior's Prayer:
Father, teach me to walk by faith and not by sight. I trust Your heart even when I can't trace Your hand. I will move forward with boldness, knowing You go before me. Lead me in Your ways today. In Jesus' name, Amen.

May 9

"Our greatest fear should not be of failure but of succeeding at things in life that don't really matter."
Francis Chan

Son,
I didn't create you to chase trophies that rust. I didn't call you to build monuments that crumble. I crafted you for eternal things. Your greatest victories will not be measured in applause, achievements, or awards—they will be measured in souls reached, hearts healed, and Kingdom ground taken.

Do not waste your life climbing ladders I never asked you to climb. Focus your life on what will matter a thousand years from now. Your hands are made to carry truth, not trophies. Your feet are made to walk paths of purpose, not popularity. Your strength is made for My mission, not man's applause. Live for eternity, son. That's where real greatness is.

"Set your minds on things above, not on earthly things."
— Colossians 3:2

Daily Challenge: Today, ask yourself before every major action: "Does this have eternal impact?" Let your decisions be shaped by eternity.

Warrior's Prayer:
Father, refocus my heart on what truly matters. Strip away anything shallow, and sharpen my hunger for eternal things. Let my life leave a mark that echoes into forever, not just today. Use me for Your Kingdom. In Jesus' name, Amen.

May 10
"We are immortal until our work on earth is done."
George Whitefield

Son,
you fear the battle.
You forget the promise.

You are immortal
until I say, "It is finished."
No sword can pierce My plan.
No storm can sink My purpose.
No enemy can erase My calling.

You are surrounded,
shielded,
sent.

Every heartbeat is assigned.
Every breath is borrowed brilliance.
Your life is not random—
it is royal.

March forward, son.
Your story is safe in My hands.

"The Lord will fulfill His purpose for me; Your steadfast love, O Lord, endures forever." — Psalm 138:8

Daily Challenge: Boldly face one fear today, remembering God holds your life securely until your mission is complete.

Warrior's Prayer:
Father, I will not fear death, disaster, or defeat. My life is Yours. My mission is Yours. Fill me with boldness to walk in my calling, unshaken and undefeated, until the day You call me home. In Jesus' name, Amen.

May 11
"Faith begins where human readiness ends."
Watchman Nee

Son,
you keep waiting to feel "ready." But I didn't call you because you were ready. I called you because you were willing. I don't need perfect resumes—I need surrendered hearts. The mission I give you isn't about your ability; it's about My power unleashed through your obedience.

I qualify you through the battlefield, not the classroom. Every step forward, every yes, every small act of obedience builds a warrior fit for greater things. Don't disqualify yourself because of weakness. That's the very space where My strength takes over. You're not just called—you're equipped. Walk like it. Fight like it. Live like it.

"Not that we are competent in ourselves to claim anything for ourselves, but our competence comes from God." — 2 Corinthians 3:5

Daily Challenge: Do one thing today you feel "unqualified" to do but know God is leading you toward. Trust His strength, not your own.

Warrior's Prayer:
Father, I lay down my insecurities and my excuses. If You have called me, You will equip me. I step forward today, not because I feel strong, but because You are strong in me. Complete Your work through my life. In Jesus' name, Amen.

May 12
"The safest place in the whole world is in the center of God's will."
Corrie ten Boom

Son,
safety isn't the absence of storms—it's My presence in the middle of them. The world tells you that safety is found in comfort, ease, and predictability. I tell you true safety is standing exactly where I placed you, no matter what rages around you.

You will feel the winds howl. You will see the waves rise. But you will not be shaken if you are anchored in Me. Don't run from the storm if I'm calling you to stand in it. I am your shield. I am your anchor. I am your safe place. Stay in My will, son, and you will find a peace no storm can touch.

"The name of the Lord is a fortified tower; the righteous run to it and are safe." — Proverbs 18:10

Daily Challenge: Identify one area where you've been seeking comfort over obedience—and today, choose obedience.

Warrior's Prayer:
Father, make my heart crave Your will more than comfort. I run to You today—my fortress, my refuge, my safe place. Anchor my soul in Your unshakable presence. In Jesus' name, Amen.

May 13
"All the darkness in the world cannot extinguish the light of a single candle."
St. Francis of Assisi

Son,
the night thickens.
Fear grows loud.
But the smallest flame
still shatters the longest night.

You were born for the battlefield.
Born for the darkness.
Born to burn bright.

Not by shouting.
Not by striving.
But by shining.

Stay close to Me.
Stay lit by My fire.
You will be the flame
hell cannot extinguish.

"The light shines in the darkness, and the darkness has not overcome it." — John 1:5

Daily Challenge: Be intentional today to bring light into a dark situation—through kindness, truth, or prayer.

Warrior's Prayer:
Father, light my life with the fire of Your Spirit. Make me a candle in the darkness, fearless and bright. Use me to ignite hope where there is despair. Shine through me today. In Jesus' name, Amen.

May 14
"God uses broken people to reach a broken world."
Nick Vujicic

Son,
you keep measuring your future by your failures. Stop. I don't recruit the flawless—I redeem the willing. Your brokenness doesn't disqualify you. It makes you usable. It humbles you, shapes you, prepares you for the real battles ahead.

I do not discard the wounded—I forge them into warriors. The cracks you fear are the very places where My glory shines through. I will build something greater from your broken pieces than you ever could from your perfection. Surrender the shame. Release the regret. Let Me use everything—even what you thought disqualified you.

"But we have this treasure in jars of clay to show that this all-surpassing power is from God and not from us."
— 2 Corinthians 4:7

Daily Challenge: Today, thank God for one area of your life that once felt like a failure—and trust Him to keep using it.

Warrior's Prayer:
Father, I bring You every broken piece of my life. Thank You for being a God who restores, redeems, and rebuilds. Use me not despite my scars, but through them. I am Yours. In Jesus' name, Amen.

May 15

*"He is no fool who gives what he cannot keep
to gain what he cannot lose."*
Jim Elliot

*Son,
your hands are too full
of what will fade.
Drop it, son.
Drop it all.*

*Your security—
your pride—
your plans.*

*Empty hands
catch eternal crowns.
Loose grip
finds unbreakable gain.*

*The world will call you reckless.
Heaven will call you wise.
Let go.
Live free.
Win forever.*

> **"Whoever wants to save their life will lose it, but whoever loses their life for Me will find it."**
> — Matthew 16:25

Daily Challenge: Identify one thing you're clinging to too tightly—and today, lay it down before God.

Warrior's Prayer:
Father, loosen my grip on what fades, and strengthen my grip on what is eternal. Teach me to trust You enough to surrender everything. Make me a man who values eternity more than earthly gain. In Jesus' name, Amen.

May 16

*"Prayer does not fit us for the greater work;
prayer is the greater work."*
Oswald Chambers

Son,
you think you're wasting time when you stop and pray. But prayer is not preparation—it's the mission itself. Every battle begins on your knees. Every victory is born in surrender. Every breakthrough happens first in unseen places before it explodes into the seen.

I am not impressed by busyness. I am moved by brokenness. Warriors who conquer the battlefield first conquer their own hearts in My presence. Don't rush ahead without hearing My voice. Don't step out without seeking My face. Prayer is your greatest weapon, your clearest strategy, your strongest armor. Fight first in the Spirit—and you will walk in power.

"The prayer of a righteous person is powerful and effective." — James 5:16

Daily Challenge: Spend at least 15 focused minutes in prayer today—no requests, just listening and surrendering.

Warrior's Prayer:
Father, teach me to fight first in prayer. Make my knees stronger than my sword arm. Let every move I make flow from time spent with You. I surrender my agenda to seek Your face above all else. In Jesus' name, Amen.

May 17
"God specializes in fresh starts and second chances."
Max Lucado

Son,
I am giving you a new beginning, not because you earned it, but because I love you. Grace is not permission to repeat the old patterns—it's power to build new ones. Don't waste the fresh soil I've placed beneath your feet by planting yesterday's weeds.

The past is paid for. The future is purchased. Today is a battlefield of choice. Step forward, not backward. Lean on My strength, not your old habits. What you sow today will echo tomorrow. Let's build something new, something eternal, something fearless. I'm with you, son. Let's begin again—with fire.

"Forget the former things; do not dwell on the past. See, I am doing a new thing!" — Isaiah 43:18–19

Daily Challenge: Identify one old habit that God is calling you to leave behind—and today, take a real action to break it.

Warrior's Prayer:
Father, thank You for new beginnings. I refuse to chain my future to my failures. By Your Spirit, I will plant new seeds of faith, obedience, and courage. Lead me forward into the new story You are writing through my life. In Jesus' name, Amen.

May 18

"The Spirit-filled life is not a special deluxe edition of Christianity. It's the standard."
A.W. Tozer

Son,
you keep swinging
an empty sword.
You keep running
on empty lungs.

Stop.

You were never meant
to fight alone.
You were built
to burn with My breath.

Powerless effort
wears you down.
Spirit-filled obedience
raises the dead.

Lay your weapons down, son.
Lift your hands up.
Let My Spirit ignite you again.

"Not by might nor by power, but by My Spirit," says the Lord Almighty. — Zechariah 4:6

Daily Challenge: Before you act today, stop and pray: "Holy Spirit, empower me. I cannot do this without You."

Warrior's Prayer:
Father, I confess I have tried to fight battles in my own strength. Fill me with Your Spirit today. Let Your power breathe through my weakness. I don't want empty effort—I want Spirit-fueled victory. In Jesus' name, Amen.

May 19
"There is no pit so deep, that God's love is not deeper still."
Betsie ten Boom

Son,
no matter how far you fall, My arms are still longer. No matter how dark the pit, My love shines deeper. There is no brokenness beyond My reach. No shame beyond My redemption. No despair beyond My resurrection.

When you hit rock bottom, you will find My hand still reaching, still redeeming, still restoring. The enemy wants you to think you are too far gone. I want you to know you are never out of My grasp. Nothing—nothing—can separate you from My love. Stop trying to climb out alone. Let Me lift you. Let Me love you back to life.

"For I am convinced that neither death nor life, neither angels nor demons… will be able to separate us from the love of God that is in Christ Jesus our Lord."
— Romans 8:38–39

Daily Challenge: Confess one area of hidden shame to God today, and ask Him to heal and restore it completely.

Warrior's Prayer:
Father, thank You that Your love goes deeper than my darkest pit. I trust You to rescue, restore, and renew what I cannot fix on my own. I surrender every broken part to You. In Jesus' name, Amen.

May 20
"When Christ calls a man, He bids him come and die."
Dietrich Bonhoeffer

Son,
the call is not to comfort.
It's to crucifixion.

Your old pride—
crucified.
Your old fears—
crucified.
Your need to be seen, praised, protected—
crucified.

Only dead men
can truly live.
Only surrendered hearts
can shake hell's gates.

I didn't call you to survive.
I called you to die
to lesser things
and rise in warrior fire.

Answer the call, son.
Lose your life—
and find it.

"I have been crucified with Christ and I no longer live, but Christ lives in me." — Galatians 2:20

Daily Challenge: Today, die to one selfish desire—and act in complete obedience to Christ instead.

Warrior's Prayer:
Father, teach me to die to myself daily, that I might live fully in You. Crucify my pride, my fears, and my selfishness. Raise me up as a warrior who lives for You alone. In Jesus' name, Amen.

May 21
"It is not your hold of Christ that saves you,
but His hold of you."
Charles Spurgeon

Son,

your grip will slip. Your strength will fail. But My hold on you will not break. Your salvation, your security, your story—none of it rests on how tightly you cling to Me. It rests on how fiercely I cling to you.

When you stumble, I will still hold you. When you question, I will still keep you. When you feel too weak to reach for Me, know that I have never stopped reaching for you. Your security is not in your perfection. It is in My promise. I will not let you go, son. Rest in My grasp. You are held—and you are home.

"I give them eternal life, and they shall never perish; no one will snatch them out of My hand." — John 10:28

Daily Challenge: Reflect today on how God has held you even through your weakest seasons. Thank Him specifically for it.

Warrior's Prayer:
Father, thank You that my salvation doesn't rest on my grip, but on Yours. Thank You for holding me when I stumble, doubt, or fail. Strengthen my trust in Your unbreakable love. I am safe in Your hands forever. In Jesus' name, Amen.

May 22

"You are the only Bible some unbelievers will ever read."
John MacArthur

Son,

your life speaks even when your mouth stays silent. People are watching—not for perfection, but for proof. Proof that grace is real. Proof that strength is possible. Proof that light can pierce even the darkest places.

You may be the only glimpse of My love someone ever sees. The way you forgive. The way you endure. The way you love the unlovable. It all matters. You're not just living for yourself—you're living for My Kingdom, on display for a world desperate for something real. Let your life shout louder than your words: Christ is alive, and He lives in you.

"Let your light shine before others, that they may see your good deeds and glorify your Father in heaven." — Matthew 5:16

Daily Challenge: Live intentionally today—ask yourself before every action: "What does my life say about Jesus?"

Warrior's Prayer:
Father, let my life preach louder than my words. Make me a living testimony of Your love, Your grace, and Your strength. Shine through me today, even when I don't realize it. In Jesus' name, Amen.

May 23
"Hardships often prepare ordinary people for an extraordinary destiny."
C.S. Lewis

Son,
you think hardship is a sign I left.
It's a sign I'm getting you ready.

Every weight strengthens.
Every wound trains.
Every tear waters a deeper root.

Heroes are not born
on easy roads.
They are built
in fire, flood, and fight.

You are not being punished.
You are being prepared.
Trust the process, son.
Your destiny is being carved
with every hammer hit.

"Consider it pure joy, my brothers and sisters, whenever you face trials of many kinds, because you know that the testing of your faith produces perseverance."
— James 1:2–3

Daily Challenge: Reframe a current hardship as preparation, not punishment. Thank God for shaping you through it.

Warrior's Prayer:
Father, give me eyes to see hardship as holy training. Build my endurance. Forge my faith. Strengthen my soul through every trial, so I am ready for the destiny You have prepared. In Jesus' name, Amen.

May 24

"Every trial is training in disguise when placed in God's hands."
Charles Stanley

Son,
I know the pain that pierced you. I know the nights you questioned if it was all meaningless. Hear Me clearly: I waste nothing. Not a tear. Not a wound. Not a single breath of suffering.

Every pain you surrender to Me becomes a weapon of grace. Every scar becomes a door of ministry. What the enemy meant for your destruction, I am turning for your destiny. Don't bury your pain—bring it to Me. I will not only heal it. I will use it to heal others. Your pain has a purpose bigger than you can imagine, son. Trust Me with it.

"And we know that in all things God works for the good of those who love Him, who have been called according to His purpose." — Romans 8:28

Daily Challenge: Write down one painful event from your past and ask God to show you how He might use it for His glory.

Warrior's Prayer:
Father, I trust You with my deepest wounds. Turn my pain into purpose, my scars into strength, and my story into a testimony. Use every broken place for Your Kingdom. In Jesus' name, Amen.

May 25

"God is more concerned with your character than your comfort."
Rick Warren

Son,
you pray for comfort.
I answer with character.

You ask for ease.
I give you endurance.

I will not pamper you, son.
I will prepare you.
I will not soften the road.
I will sharpen your resolve.

Because I love you,
I will let the hard things
shape holy things.

Do not fear the chiseling.
It is the mark of a Master Craftsman.

You are being carved
for something eternal.

"No discipline seems pleasant at the time, but painful. Later on, however, it produces a harvest of righteousness and peace." — Hebrews 12:11

Daily Challenge: Endure one difficult situation today without complaining—thank God for shaping you through it.

Warrior's Prayer:
Father, don't let me run from the hard things that build holy character. Shape me, chisel me, refine me. I trust Your hand even when it hurts. Make me a man of righteousness and peace. In Jesus' name, Amen.

May 26

"God's promises are like the stars; the darker the night, the brighter they shine."
David Nicholas

Son,
when the night gets darker, remember: My promises don't fade—they glow. When the ground shakes, remember: My Word is more stable than the mountains. When your strength fails, remember: My promises carry more weight than your fears.

I didn't promise an easy path—I promised a faithful presence. I didn't promise you would always see the way clearly—I promised you would never walk it alone. In the darkest night, My promises shine the brightest. Look up, son. Fix your eyes not on the storm, but on the stars of My faithfulness. Hold fast. Morning is coming.

"The Lord is trustworthy in all He promises and faithful in all He does." — Psalm 145:13

Daily Challenge: Memorize a Bible promise today and speak it aloud whenever fear or doubt creep in.

Warrior's Prayer:
Father, thank You for promises that shine brighter than any darkness. Help me fix my eyes on Your truth when fear whispers lies. I stand today anchored in Your faithfulness. In Jesus' name, Amen.

May 27

*"Faith is taking the first step even when you
don't see the whole staircase."*
Martin Luther King Jr.

Son,

you're waiting for clarity. I'm waiting for obedience. I don't light up the whole staircase—I light up the next step. You don't need to see the end of the story to trust the next sentence I'm writing.

Faith isn't fueled by sight—it's fueled by surrender. I'm not asking you to control the future; I'm asking you to trust Me with it. Take the step, even if your knees shake. Move forward when your mind still questions. I am already waiting at the top, son. One step of obedience at a time— that's how you will walk into your destiny.

"Your word is a lamp to my feet and a light to my path."
— Psalm 119:105

Daily Challenge: Take one small step today in an area where fear or uncertainty has held you back.

Warrior's Prayer:
Father, even when I can't see the whole way, I will take the next step by faith. Light my path, strengthen my heart, and remind me that You are already at the finish line. I walk by trust, not by sight. In Jesus' name, Amen.

May 28

*"Satan trembles when he sees the weakest
saint upon his knees."*
William Cowper

*Son,
you think the enemy fears your strength.
He fears your surrender.*

*He does not tremble
when you flex.
He trembles
when you kneel.*

*Because when you bow before Me,
you rise in a power
no demon can defeat.*

*Prayer is not preparation for battle—
it is the battle.*

*Kneel low, son.
Rise unstoppable.*

"Submit yourselves, then, to God. Resist the devil, and he will flee from you." — James 4:7

Daily Challenge: Spend 10 minutes today in focused prayer, asking God to fight battles you cannot win on your own.

Warrior's Prayer:
Father, teach me the power of surrender. Drive me to my knees so I can rise in victory. Fight my battles as I submit fully to You. I trust Your strength, not my own. In Jesus' name, Amen.

May 29
"Our hearts are restless until they rest in You."
St. Augustine

Son,
the unrest you feel isn't solved by success. It isn't silenced by distractions. The ache inside you can only be healed by My presence. True peace is not the absence of problems—it's the presence of Me.

Stop chasing stillness from the outside in. I designed you to find your calm from the inside out—anchored in Me. No storm can steal it. No failure can shake it. No enemy can break it. Draw near to Me, son. When your heart is tangled in anxiety, don't run faster. Run to Me. I am your peace.

"You will keep in perfect peace those whose minds are steadfast, because they trust in You." — Isaiah 26:3

Daily Challenge: When anxiety rises today, immediately stop and pray: "Father, center me in Your peace."

Warrior's Prayer:
Father, You are my peace in every storm, my calm in every chaos. Teach me to run to You first and anchor my mind in Your truth. Fill me with Your unshakable peace today. In Jesus' name, Amen.

May 30
"Earth has no sorrow that heaven cannot heal."
Thomas Moore

Son,
the wounds you hide
I see.
The grief you carry
I know.
The weight you bear
I bore first.

There is no cut
so deep
that My hands cannot heal.
No sorrow
so heavy
that My shoulders cannot carry.

Bring Me the shattered pieces.
Bring Me the heavy sighs.
I am the Healer, son.
I make graves into gardens.

"He heals the brokenhearted and binds up their wounds." — Psalm 147:3

Daily Challenge: Confess one hidden hurt to God today—and trust Him to begin the healing process.

Warrior's Prayer:
Father, I give You the wounds I try to hide. Heal my heart. Bind up my broken places. I trust You to turn sorrow into strength, mourning into dancing. Complete Your healing work in me. In Jesus' name, Amen.

May 31

"God never said the journey would be easy, but He did say the arrival would be worthwhile."
Max Lucado

Son,
you weren't promised a smooth road. You were promised a victorious ending. There will be days when you feel bruised, bloodied, and exhausted. Days when you wonder if it's worth it. Hear Me now: It is.

Every battle has a purpose. Every scar tells a story of My faithfulness. Every step taken in obedience is a declaration of war against darkness. The finish line is real—and it's glorious beyond what you can imagine. Keep moving, son. When you can't run, crawl. When you can't stand, lean into Me. You will finish this race—and it will be worth every cost.

"I have fought the good fight, I have finished the race, I have kept the faith." — 2 Timothy 4:7

Daily Challenge: Push through one hard thing today, reminding yourself: "This race is worth it."

Warrior's Prayer:
Father, strengthen my resolve to finish the race You have set before me. When I'm weary, be my strength. When I'm discouraged, be my hope. I run for Your glory—and I will not quit. In Jesus' name, Amen.

June 1
"When you can't trace God's hand, trust His heart."
Charles Spurgeon

Son,
when it feels like you have nothing left, that's where I do My deepest work. When the walls close in and your strength runs dry, you are finally positioned for a miracle. I am not limited by your resources. I am not confined by your abilities. I specialize in creating rivers in the wasteland and beauty from ashes.

Your nothing is the perfect stage for My everything. Trust Me when you feel empty. That's when I am about to fill you in ways you never imagined. Keep your eyes up, son. I do My best work when you think all is lost.

"Behold, I am doing a new thing; now it springs forth, do you not perceive it? I will make a way in the wilderness and rivers in the desert." — Isaiah 43:19

Daily Challenge: When you feel empty today, pray: "God, I trust You to work even here."

Warrior's Prayer:
Father, when I have nothing left to give, fill me with Your power. When I am weakest, show Your strength. I trust You to work miracles in the wilderness of my life. I lift my eyes to You. In Jesus' name, Amen.

June 2

"Christ is not valued at all until He is valued above all."
Augustine of Hippo

Son,
you are looking
for more strength,
more answers,
more control.

Stop searching.
Start seeing.

You already have
all you need—
Me.

My presence is enough.
My promises are enough.
My love is enough.

Hold onto Me, son.
You lack nothing.

"The Lord is my shepherd; I lack nothing."
— Psalm 23:1

Daily Challenge: List three ways God has already provided for you—and thank Him for each.

Warrior's Prayer:
Father, remind me today that Your presence is enough. I will not live in scarcity when I walk with the God of abundance. Fill my heart with gratitude and contentment. In Jesus' name, Amen.

June 3

*"Worship puts God in the center and
everything else in its place."*
Louie Giglio

Son,
your fear grows when you stare at the storm. Your strength grows when you stare at Me. Whatever you focus on fills your heart. Focus on fear—you'll be ruled by it. Focus on My power—you'll rise above it.

Lift your eyes, son. I am bigger than the mountain, stronger than the enemy, louder than the lies. Fix your mind on My faithfulness, and you will walk in peace even when the earth shakes. Shift your gaze—and you will shift your battle.

"You will keep in perfect peace those whose minds are steadfast, because they trust in You." — Isaiah 26:3

Daily Challenge: Catch yourself today every time your mind spirals in fear—and immediately redirect your focus to God's promises.

Warrior's Prayer:
Father, train my eyes to stay fixed on You, not on fear. Help me see Your strength when the storm rises. Keep me anchored in peace because I trust You more than anything I face. In Jesus' name, Amen.

June 4

"Every warrior is trained in resistance – not ease."
John Bevere

Son,
you pray for strength—
then resist the strain.
You pray for wisdom—
then shrink from the weight.

Growth is not born
on easy paths.
It is forged
through pressure,
through stretching,
through surrender.

Lean into the discomfort, son.
That is where the roots dig deeper.
That is where the muscles are built.

Pain is not punishment.
It's preparation.

"Consider it pure joy, my brothers and sisters, whenever you face trials of many kinds, because you know that the testing of your faith produces perseverance."
— James 1:2–3

Daily Challenge: Embrace one uncomfortable moment today as a chance for growth—don't resist it, lean into it.

Warrior's Prayer:
Father, help me stop running from the stretching You are doing in my life. Use discomfort to deepen my roots and build my strength. I trust You are growing something eternal in me. In Jesus' name, Amen.

June 5

"The smallest act of obedience in faith is greater than the grandest plan."
A.W. Tozer

Son,
the world will measure you by results. I measure you by obedience. When you stand before Me, I won't ask if you were the most successful—I'll ask if you were the most faithful.

Stop chasing results. Start chasing My voice. Trust that even when you don't see immediate fruit, every step of obedience is building an eternal harvest. Stay the course, son. Obey when it's hard. Obey when it's hidden. Obey when no one sees. That's where real greatness is born.

"To obey is better than sacrifice, and to heed is better than the fat of rams." — 1 Samuel 15:22

Daily Challenge: Take one small act of obedience today, even if no one notices—do it for God's eyes alone.

Warrior's Prayer:
Father, make me a man who values obedience over outcome. Strengthen my resolve to follow You even when I don't see the results yet. Let my faithfulness bring You glory. In Jesus' name, Amen.

June 6
"We are not called to be safe, but to be sent."
David Livingstone

Son,
comfort zones are where dreams die. I didn't call you to stay safe—I called you to step out. I called you to climb mountains, to face giants, to blaze trails where fear tried to build walls.

Faith is forged on the front lines, not the sidelines. Courage isn't the absence of fear—it's moving forward in spite of it, knowing I go before you. Don't settle for survival when I made you for battle. Take the step, son. I'm with you in the risk. I'm with you in the roar. I'm with you in the fight.

"Have I not commanded you? Be strong and courageous. Do not be afraid; do not be discouraged, for the Lord your God will be with you wherever you go."
— Joshua 1:9

Daily Challenge: Take a bold step today that stretches you out of your comfort zone for God's glory.

Warrior's Prayer:
Father, I reject the temptation to live safe. Fill me with courage to step into the unknown, trusting Your strength more than my fear. Lead me where only the brave can go. In Jesus' name, Amen.

June 7

"Hardships often prepare ordinary people for an extraordinary destiny."
C.S. Lewis

Son,
pain screams.
Purpose whispers.

The pain says quit.
The purpose says continue.

You are not abandoned in the hurt.
You are being anointed in the fire.

The greater the crushing,
the greater the calling.
The deeper the pain,
the higher the purpose.

Hold on, son.
The plan is bigger
than the pain.

"And we know that in all things God works for the good of those who love Him, who have been called according to His purpose." — Romans 8:28

Daily Challenge: When pain hits today, whisper this: "God's plan is greater than my pain."

Warrior's Prayer:
Father, when pain presses in, anchor me in Your purpose. Remind me that You are working good even when I can't see it. Strengthen me to trust the process. In Jesus' name, Amen.

June 8
"We don't fight for victory. We fight from the victory Jesus already won."
Tony Evans

Son,
you are not a desperate soldier hoping to win—you are a victorious warrior enforcing what I have already won. The cross wasn't a temporary victory; it was the final declaration of triumph.

You don't have to wonder if you'll make it—you fight from a place of guaranteed victory. When you feel weak, remember: the battle is already decided. Your job is to stand, to fight, and to finish strong because the war is already won in My name.

Fight from victory, not for it, son. You already wear the crown.

"But thanks be to God! He gives us the victory through our Lord Jesus Christ." — 1 Corinthians 15:57

Daily Challenge: Today, face a challenge with the mindset: "This battle is already won in Jesus."

Warrior's Prayer:
Father, thank You that I fight from victory, not for it. Strengthen my spirit to stand firm and live as a conqueror through Christ. Remind me daily that the war is already won. In Jesus' name, Amen.

June 9

"The first act of faith is obedience."
Dietrich Bonhoeffer

Son,
waiting for breakthrough?
Start with obedience.

Dreaming of destiny?
Start with surrender.

The doors you're begging Me to open
swing on the hinges of your obedience.

Not louder prayers.
Not bigger promises.
Just simple, fierce obedience.

Obey when it's easy.
Obey when it's costly.
Obey when no one claps.

That's where the miracles live.

"If you are willing and obedient, you shall eat the good of the land." — Isaiah 1:19

Daily Challenge: Obey God quickly in one area today—even if it's hard or inconvenient.

Warrior's Prayer:
Father, make me a man who obeys You without hesitation. Teach me that delayed obedience is still disobedience. I want to unlock everything You have for me through fearless surrender. In Jesus' name, Amen.

June 10

"I've learned to kiss the wave that throws me against the Rock of Ages."
Charles Spurgeon

Son,
the mountain you're facing feels immovable—but I'm greater still. I don't always move the mountain out of the way. Sometimes I strengthen you to climb it. Sometimes I teach you to conquer it. Either way, I am with you every step.

Don't be intimidated by the size of the obstacle. Be anchored by the size of your God. This moment may seem massive—but it will fall in the face of faith. One step of obedience, one word of trust, one act of boldness at a time—you will move forward through it.

"Truly I tell you, if you have faith as small as a mustard seed, you can say to this mountain, 'Move from here to there,' and it will move." — Matthew 17:20

Daily Challenge: Speak faith today over a situation that feels impossible—declare God's power over it.

Warrior's Prayer:
Father, the mountain in front of me is nothing compared to the strength behind me. Strengthen my faith to speak boldly, walk bravely, and trust deeply. Move through me to move the impossible. In Jesus' name, Amen.

June 11
"The silence of God is not the absence of God."
Elisabeth Elliot

Son,
silence is not absence.
Stillness is not abandonment.
I am always working, always speaking—sometimes louder in whispers than in shouts.

When you don't feel Me, trust My promises. When you don't hear Me, cling to what I already said. My silence is not a shutdown—it's a strengthening. It's in the quiet that your faith matures, your roots dig deep, and your heart learns to walk by trust instead of sight.

You are not forgotten. You are being fortified.

"Be still, and know that I am God." — Psalm 46:10

Daily Challenge: Spend five minutes in absolute silence before God today—no requests, just stillness.

Warrior's Prayer:
Father, when I can't hear You, I will trust that You are near. Strengthen my faith in the silence. Teach me to find Your heart even when my ears are empty. I rest in Your unseen work. In Jesus' name, Amen.

June 12
*"The greatness of a man's power is the
measure of his surrender."*
William Booth

Son,
you wonder why
the battle chose you.

It didn't.

I chose you
for the battle.

You were built
for this war.
You were designed
for these days.

Not to merely survive—
but to lead,
to stand,
to overcome.

You are not a victim.
You are My warrior.

Rise, son.
This is your hour.

"But you, take courage! Do not let your hands be weak, for your work shall be rewarded." — 2 Chronicles 15:7

Daily Challenge: Stand firm today where you've been tempted to give up—declare, "I was built for this."

Warrior's Prayer:
Father, You have equipped me for the battles I face. Strengthen my hands. Sharpen my focus. Help me rise and fight with confidence, knowing You chose me for this time. In Jesus' name, Amen.

June 13
"A ship is safe in harbor, but that's not what ships are built for."
John A. Shedd

Son,
you were not built to stay docked in safety. You were crafted to brave deep waters, to sail into storms, and to carry My mission to distant shores. Playing it safe was never your calling.

There is Kingdom ground that will only be taken if you leave the harbor. Fear will chain you to the dock—but faith will push you to set sail. Trust My wind to fill your sails. Trust My compass to guide your steps. I didn't create you to float—I created you to conquer.

> **"Launch out into the deep, and let down your nets for a catch."** — Luke 5:4

Daily Challenge: Identify one area today where you're playing it safe—and take one bold step forward instead.

Warrior's Prayer:
Father, break the chains of fear that keep me docked in comfort. Launch me into deeper waters where Your glory is revealed. I trust Your hand to guide and sustain me. In Jesus' name, Amen.

June 14

"The prayerful man is the most powerful man."
E.M. Bounds

Son,
you think the strongest warrior
is the one who stands tallest.

But the mightiest move
is the one who kneels first.

Strength that resists Me
breaks.
Strength that surrenders to Me
builds nations.

Your knees
are your battlefield.
Your surrender
is your sword.

Bow low, son.
Rise invincible.

"Humble yourselves before the Lord, and He will lift you up." — James 4:10

Daily Challenge: Surrender one thing today you've been stubbornly holding onto—and lay it fully before God.

Warrior's Prayer:
Father, I surrender every part of my life to You—my plans, my dreams, my fears. I trust Your way over my own. Make my surrender my strongest weapon. In Jesus' name, Amen.

June 15

"Character is what you are in the dark."
D.L. Moody

Son,
I see the battles you fight in secret. I see the nights you wrestle in prayer, the temptations you resist when no one is watching, the burdens you carry quietly for others. Nothing escapes My notice.

The private victories matter as much as the public ones. I reward what is done in secret. Every hidden obedience echoes loudly in My Kingdom. Keep fighting the unseen fights, son. They are building an unshakable legacy.

"Then your Father, who sees what is done in secret, will reward you." — Matthew 6:6

Daily Challenge: Celebrate a private victory today that no one else knows about—and give God the glory.

Warrior's Prayer:
Father, thank You for seeing every unseen battle I fight. Strengthen me to stay faithful even when no one notices. Help me live for Your applause alone. In Jesus' name, Amen.

June 16

*"God is never late. His delays are not denials.
They are a preparation."*
Corrie ten Boom

Son,

waiting isn't wasting. It's warfare. While you wait, I am moving in ways your eyes can't see. I am preparing people, positioning opportunities, strengthening your heart for what's coming.

Don't despise the delay. Use it. Let waiting refine your trust, not rot your faith. I am not late. I am not absent. I am orchestrating a victory that will be worth every second you stood in patience. Wait with your head high, son. Warriors who wait on Me never lose ground—they gain strength.

"But they who wait for the Lord shall renew their strength; they shall mount up with wings like eagles."
— Isaiah 40:31

Daily Challenge: Today, thank God for something you're still waiting for instead of complaining about it.

Warrior's Prayer:
Father, teach me to wait with expectation, not frustration. Strengthen me as I stand still. Remind me You are always working, even when I can't see it. I trust Your timing. In Jesus' name, Amen.

June 17

*"Don't just be willing to fight for truth.
Be willing to bleed for it."
Richard Wurmbrand*

*Son,
you avoid the giant,
thinking delay is victory.*

It's not.

*The battles you ignore
grow stronger.
The fears you bury
grow deeper.*

*Face it, son.
Call it out.
Step onto the battlefield.*

*I have already armed you.
I have already assured you.*

*Victory waits
on the other side of confrontation.*

"The Lord will fight for you; you need only to be still."
— Exodus 14:14

Daily Challenge: Identify one fear you've been avoiding—and today, face it head-on with prayer and boldness.

Warrior's Prayer:
Father, I will not hide from my battles. Give me courage to confront what I have feared, knowing You fight with me and for me. Strengthen my spirit today. In Jesus' name, Amen.

June 18
"Disappointments are His appointments."
C.H. Spurgeon

Son,
I know it hurts when doors slam shut. I know you wonder why dreams collapse. But hear Me: sometimes I wreck your plans because I'm protecting a bigger purpose. I'm not trying to punish you—I'm positioning you.

You don't see the traps I'm steering you away from. You don't see the miracles I'm setting up. Trust Me when I say "no." Trust Me when the map falls apart. I am not wrecking your life—I'm rescuing it. My plans for you are still good, still unstoppable, still unfolding.

"For I know the plans I have for you, declares the Lord, plans to prosper you and not to harm you, plans to give you hope and a future." — Jeremiah 29:11

Daily Challenge: Let go of one broken plan today—and surrender it completely to God's greater purpose.

Warrior's Prayer:
Father, even when I don't understand, I choose to trust You. Wreck whatever needs wrecked to rescue what needs saving. Align my heart with Your will, not just my own. In Jesus' name, Amen.

June 19
"The battle is not yours, but God's."
2 Chronicles 20:15

Son,
you fight battles
you were never meant to carry.

You wrestle shadows
when I already declared the light.

The battle is not yours
to win alone.

It is Mine.
It has always been Mine.

Drop your sword,
lift your hands,
and watch Me fight for you.

You are not defeated.
You are defended.

"The Lord your God is the one who goes with you to fight for you against your enemies to give you victory."
— Deuteronomy 20:4

Daily Challenge: Hand over one battle you're carrying today—surrender it fully to God's hands.

Warrior's Prayer:
Father, I lay down my sword today and trust You to fight for me. Strengthen my faith to watch You work in ways I never could on my own. The battle is Yours—and so is the victory. In Jesus' name, Amen.

June 20

"The true test of a man's character is what he does when no one is watching."
John Wooden

Son,
talent can open doors, but only character keeps them open. I'm not just shaping your skills—I'm forging your soul. Integrity is the armor you wear when no one is watching. Purity is the sword you carry when temptation attacks.

Don't just be impressive—be immovable. Let your strength be measured not by how loudly you roar but by how deeply you stand rooted in Me. When others crumble under pressure, you will stand firm because you were built in the secret places where no spotlight shines. Character will carry you farther than charisma ever could.

"The integrity of the upright guides them, but the unfaithful are destroyed by their duplicity."
— Proverbs 11:3

Daily Challenge: Focus today on one hidden area of your life—and choose character over compromise.

Warrior's Prayer:
Father, build my character stronger than my reputation. Make my roots deeper than my talents. Forge in me a man of integrity, courage, and relentless obedience to You. In Jesus' name, Amen.

June 21
"The best is yet to come."
Corrie ten Boom

Son,
if you're still breathing, you're still called. Your past failures didn't cancel your purpose. Your mistakes didn't erase your mission. I'm not finished with you. Far from it—I'm just getting started.

The enemy wants you to think it's over. I'm telling you it's time to rise. There is still ground to take. Still battles to fight. Still victories to claim. As long as there's breath in your lungs, there's fire in your calling. Get up, son. It's not over. It's just beginning.

"Being confident of this, that He who began a good work in you will carry it on to completion until the day of Christ Jesus." — Philippians 1:6

Daily Challenge: Declare today: "God's not done with me." Then take one bold step in the direction of your calling.

Warrior's Prayer:
Father, thank You that You are never finished writing my story. I refuse to quit. Strengthen my spirit to keep moving, keep fighting, and keep trusting until my mission is complete. In Jesus' name, Amen.

June 22

"The stars may fall, but God's promises will stand and be fulfilled."
J.I. Packer

Son,
the waves roar,
the winds scream,
and your knees shake.

But listen:
the storm does not decide your story.
I do.

Lift your head,
square your shoulders,
and speak to the storm.

Not with fear.
Not with retreat.

With authority.
With fire.
With faith.

Your God is bigger
than anything trying to break you.

"He got up, rebuked the wind and said to the waves, 'Quiet! Be still!' Then the wind died down and it was completely calm." — Mark 4:39

Daily Challenge: Speak a bold prayer today over a situation that feels out of control. Command fear to be still in Jesus' name.

Warrior's Prayer:
Father, You are bigger than every storm I face. Teach me to speak with the authority You've given me. Calm my spirit and strengthen my stand. I trust You to silence the chaos. In Jesus' name, Amen.

June 23

"You are not what you think you are,
but what you think-you are."
Norman Vincent Peale

Son,
your thoughts are not harmless. They are the battlefield where wars are won or lost. What fills your mind will eventually fill your mouth, your hands, and your heart.

If you dwell on fear, you'll live paralyzed. If you feast on lies, you'll walk in defeat. But if you fix your mind on My truth, you'll walk in freedom. You have the power to choose what you feed your spirit. Feed it with faith. Feed it with My Word. Starve the lies. Fuel the fire.

"Set your minds on things above, not on earthly things."
— Colossians 3:2

Daily Challenge: Catch every negative thought today—and replace it immediately with a promise from Scripture.

Warrior's Prayer:
Father, guard my mind today. Help me take every thought captive and make it obedient to Christ. Fill my heart with Your truth and crowd out every lie. Shape my life through the power of Your Word. In Jesus' name, Amen.

June 24

"There is more mercy in Christ than sin in us."
Richard Sibbes

Son,
the enemy calls you by your past.
I call you by your purpose.

He wants you chained
to memories.
I want you launched
into destiny.

Grace does not erase your story.
It redeems it.

Every scar—
a sentence of strength.
Every failure—
a doorway to deeper faith.

You are not marked by shame, son.
You are branded by grace.

"Where sin increased, grace increased all the more."
— Romans 5:20

Daily Challenge: Reflect today on one past failure—and thank God for how He has used it to build you stronger.

Warrior's Prayer:
Father, thank You for grace that rewrites my story. I refuse to live under shame when You have called me free. Redeem every part of my past for Your glory. In Jesus' name, Amen.

June 25
"Though He slay me, yet will I hope in Him."
Job 13:15

Son,
it feels like you've been buried—forgotten, crushed, hidden. But you are not buried to die. You are planted to grow.

In the dark, roots are taking hold. In the silence, strength is building. In the hidden place, purpose is being shaped. You are not stuck—you are being seeded for a greater harvest. Trust the season. What feels like death is the beginning of new life. Stay rooted in Me, son. The breakthrough is coming.

"Very truly I tell you, unless a kernel of wheat falls to the ground and dies, it remains only a single seed. But if it dies, it produces many seeds." — John 12:24

Daily Challenge: Embrace the hidden work God is doing in your life today—pray: "Father, grow me even here."

Warrior's Prayer:
Father, when it feels like nothing is happening, remind me You are working underground. Strengthen my roots. Build my faith. Prepare me for the harvest You have planted me to produce. In Jesus' name, Amen.

June 26

"Faith is to believe what you do not see; the reward of this faith is to see what you believe."
St. Augustine

Son,

I'm not just able—I'm faithful. I'm not just powerful—I'm personal. You don't have to wonder if I can move; you need to believe I will move according to My perfect plan.

Faith isn't wishful thinking. It's anchored assurance. I am not a distant God hoping you make it—I am the Warrior King guaranteeing your victory. Don't shrink back. Step up. Stand firm. Speak My promises louder than your fears. Your faith activates mountains to move.

"Now faith is the assurance of things hoped for, the conviction of things not seen." — Hebrews 11:1

Daily Challenge: Boldly declare one promise of God today over your life as if it's already done.

Warrior's Prayer:
Father, anchor my heart in full assurance of who You are. Teach me to walk by faith, not by sight. Let my words, my steps, and my battles be marked by bold trust in You. In Jesus' name, Amen.

June 27

*"God uses men who are weak and feeble
enough to lean on Him."*
Hudson Taylor

Son,
you think brokenness
disqualifies you.

It doesn't.

It positions you.

The cracks in your armor
let My glory shine through.
The scars on your heart
become blueprints for healing others.

I don't need your perfection, son.
I need your permission.

Permission to use the broken places.
Permission to breathe life into the ashes.

You are not too shattered
to be sent.

You are exactly who I chose.

"But we have this treasure in jars of clay to show that this all-surpassing power is from God and not from us."
— 2 Corinthians 4:7

Daily Challenge: Embrace one broken place today as part of your testimony—thank God for how He's using it.

Warrior's Prayer:
Father, I surrender my brokenness into Your hands. Use my scars to tell Your story. Use my cracks to reveal Your light. I am Yours. In Jesus' name, Amen.

June 28
"God delights in impossibilities."
Andrew Murray

Son,
what looks impossible to you is easy for Me. The sea was never the barrier—the doubt was. I didn't bring you this far to leave you stranded.

I am still the God who splits oceans, topples giants, crumbles walls, and raises the dead. Trust My power, not your perspective. What stands in front of you today is already subject to My command. Lift your faith higher than your fear. Watch what I will do.

"The Lord will fight for you; you need only to be still."
— Exodus 14:14

Daily Challenge: Pray boldly over one "impossible" situation today—and expect God to move powerfully.

Warrior's Prayer:
Father, I believe You are the same miracle-working God today. Part the seas before me. Make a way where there is no way. Strengthen my faith to trust You for the impossible. In Jesus' name, Amen.

June 29

"We are to praise God even when the world is falling apart-especially then."
Elisabeth Elliot

Son,
when hell rages,
don't just fight—
worship.

When fear roars,
don't just run—
praise.

Praise breaks chains.
Praise shatters walls.
Praise invites My power
into the battlefield.

Lift your voice, son.
Not when it's easy—
especially when it's not.

Praise is your sword.
Praise is your shield.
Praise is your war cry.

Use it.

"I will bless the Lord at all times; His praise shall continually be in my mouth." — Psalm 34:1

Daily Challenge: When pressure hits today, stop and praise God out loud for who He is.

Warrior's Prayer:
Father, teach me to fight with praise. Fill my mouth with worship even when I'm under fire. Let my praise shift the atmosphere and invite Your victory into every battle. In Jesus' name, Amen.

June 30
*"When you come to the end of your rope,
tie a knot and hang on."*
Franklin D. Roosevelt

Son,

the pressure intensifies right before breakthrough. The night feels darkest just before the dawn. Don't let the enemy convince you to give up when you're on the brink of victory.

You are closer than you know. One more prayer. One more step. One more act of obedience. The finish line is just ahead. Keep swinging the sword. Keep holding the line. Keep marching in faith. I am with you, son—and I never lose. Finish strong.

"Let us not grow weary in doing good, for at the proper time we will reap a harvest if we do not give up." —
Galatians 6:9

Daily Challenge: Push through one thing today that feels heavy—remind yourself: "I'm closer than I think."

Warrior's Prayer:
Father, fuel my spirit to finish strong. When I'm weary, strengthen my hands. When I'm tempted to quit, renew my vision. I trust You for the breakthrough. I will not stop short. In Jesus' name, Amen.

July 1

"Outside of the will of God, there's nothing I want. Inside the will of God, there's nothing I fear."
A.W. Tozer

Son,
My will isn't a trap—it's a shield. My path isn't a burden—it's a battle plan for victory. When you walk outside of My will, you are exposed to attacks you were never built to fight. But when you walk inside of My will, you are armored, armed, and anointed.

Following Me doesn't mean the road will be easy. It means it will be meaningful. It means every step will matter. Every scar will have a purpose. Every tear will water a harvest. You were not made to drift through life hoping for comfort—you were designed to charge forward in My calling, fearless, because you know the One leading you cannot fail.

Stay anchored to My voice, son. The will of God is the safest, strongest, fiercest place you can live. And I will never leave your side.

"Your word is a lamp to my feet and a light to my path."
— Psalm 119:105

Daily Challenge: Surrender your plans today. Say it out loud: "Father, burn away every desire not rooted in Your will."

Warrior's Prayer:
Father, I want nothing outside of You. Break every chain of selfish ambition in my heart. Forge my spirit to love Your will more than my comfort. Lead me, command me, and strengthen me to follow wherever You call. I will not fear the road when I walk it with You. In Jesus' name, Amen.

July 2

*"A faith that cannot be tested is a faith
that cannot be trusted."*
Adrian Rogers

Son,
you pray for stronger faith, but you flinch at the furnace. Understand this: I strengthen faith the same way fire strengthens steel—by exposing weakness, burning off impurities, and forging something unbreakable.

Faith grows through the trial, not the triumph. It's not forged in ease but in the crushing moments where you have to choose Me over fear, obedience over comfort, worship over worry. Every test is not just a fight for survival—it's an invitation to become a warrior who walks with Me through fire without the smell of smoke.

I am not setting you up to fail. I am setting you up to stand. Trust Me in the test, son. When you come through it, you won't just survive—you'll shine.

"The testing of your faith produces perseverance."
— James 1:3

Daily Challenge: Look at one trial today and declare: "This is building my unshakable faith."

Warrior's Prayer:
Father, when the fire comes, make my faith fiercer, not weaker. Strip away anything that cannot survive the heat. Strengthen my endurance, sharpen my trust, and forge me into a man who is dangerous to the darkness. I embrace the test, because I trust the Teacher. In Jesus' name, Amen.

July 3
"God gives His hardest battles to His strongest soldiers."
Unknown

Son,
you cry out,
"Why this battle?
Why now?
Why me?"

Because I see in you
what you cannot yet see.

I see the iron under the skin.
I see the flame that fear cannot smother.
I see the lion I am awakening.

I chose you, son.
Not because you are flawless—
but because you are faithful.

Not because you are perfect—
but because you are willing.

The fiercest fights
are handed to the fiercest warriors.

You are not forgotten.
You are trusted.

Hold the line.
You were born for this hour.

"Endure hardship as discipline; God is treating you as His children." — Hebrews 12:7

Daily Challenge: Face today's hardships with this mindset. "God trusted me with this battle."

Warrior's Prayer:
Father, when the fight feels overwhelming, remind me You trusted me with this mission. Strengthen my spine. Ignite my heart. Steady my hands for war. I will not shrink back—I will rise. Because You are with me. In Jesus' name, Amen.

July 4
"Freedom is never free."
Ronald Reagan

Son,
the freedom you enjoy—spiritually, mentally, and even physically—was bought at a brutal price. Freedom cost blood. Freedom demanded sacrifice. Freedom demanded courage from those willing to stand when others fled.

Never forget the cross that purchased your ultimate freedom. Never forget the warriors who paved the way for your earthly freedoms. Freedom is a gift—but it's also a responsibility. I didn't set you free to sit still or live small. I set you free to advance My Kingdom with reckless courage and unwavering truth.

Don't squander your freedom trying to please the world. Spend it setting captives free. Spend it waging war for the souls still bound in chains. You are free, son. Now fight like it.

"It is for freedom that Christ has set us free. Stand firm, then, and do not let yourselves be burdened again by a yoke of slavery." — Galatians 5:1

Daily Challenge: Do one bold act today that honors the freedom Christ died to give you.

Warrior's Prayer:
Father, thank You for the freedom that cost everything. I will not live shackled when You have called me to be free. Use my life as a weapon to break chains, not just for myself but for others. I will fight for freedom with every breath You give me. In Jesus' name, Amen.

July 5

*"God brings men into deep waters not to drown them,
but to cleanse them."*
James H. Aughey

Son,
the story you wish you could erase is the story I am eager to tell. Every broken moment, every desperate prayer, every comeback you didn't think you could survive—it all weaves a testimony of power that hell cannot silence.

There are people you haven't met yet whose lives will be changed by the chapters you thought disqualified you. Your scars are not shameful. They are signs of survival. Of My grace. Of My resurrection power at work inside you.

Don't hide your story, son. Speak it. Live it. Let it roar. It is My glory written across your life for the world to see.

"Let the redeemed of the Lord tell their story—those He redeemed from the hand of the foe." — Psalm 107:2

Daily Challenge: Find one opportunity today to share even a small piece of your story—and trust God to use it.

Warrior's Prayer:
Father, thank You for redeeming every broken chapter of my story. Give me boldness to share my scars as signs of Your victory. Let my life become a weapon of hope for those still in chains. I will not be silent about what You have done. In Jesus' name, Amen.

July 6

*"Prayer is not overcoming God's reluctance,
but laying hold of His willingness."*
Martin Luther

Son,
you don't have to twist My arm to bless you. You don't have to beg Me to love you. You don't have to convince Me to be good to you. I was willing long before you ever whispered a prayer.

Prayer isn't about forcing My hand. It's about aligning your heart. It's about stepping into the flood of grace that is already rushing toward you. I am a Father who wants to be found. A King who wants to fight for His sons. Prayer is your access point to the strength, wisdom, and power I've already poured out.

Kneel boldly. Speak boldly. Expect boldly. I am listening.

"Call to Me and I will answer you and tell you great and unsearchable things you do not know." — Jeremiah 33:3

Daily Challenge: Spend at least 15 minutes today in prayer—no agenda, just connection and surrender.

Warrior's Prayer:
Father, I approach You not as a beggar but as a beloved son. Align my heart with Yours. Fill me with boldness to ask, seek, and knock—trusting that You are good beyond my wildest prayers. In Jesus' name, Amen.

July 7

"You were made by God and for God, and until you understand that, life will never make sense."
Rick Warren

Son,

you were not an accident. You were not random. You are not here to simply survive another day. I crafted you for war, for worship, for wonder. Your life is a weapon in My hands, not a mistake to be hidden away.

Everything you seek outside of Me will leave you hollow. Every path you chase without Me will leave you wandering. Come back to your origin, son. You were made by Me—for Me. When you root yourself in that truth, every moment begins to pulse with eternal purpose.

You were born for something bigger than comfort. You were born for Me.

"For in Him we live and move and have our being."
— Acts 17:28

Daily Challenge: Remind yourself throughout the day: "I was made for God's glory, not my own comfort."

Warrior's Prayer:
Father, plant this truth deep into my heart—I was made by You and for You. Strip away anything in my life that chases smaller purposes. I surrender fully to Your calling today. In Jesus' name, Amen.

July 8

"What you do when you don't have to will determine what you'll be when you can't help it."
Oswald Chambers

Son,
the silent battles
matter most.

The fights you face alone—
the temptations you resist in the dark,
the doubts you defeat in the night,
the tears you shed where no one claps.

I see them all.

The world crowns the visible victories.
I reward the secret ones.

Every unseen stand you make
is building a legacy hell cannot erase.

Keep fighting, son.
I am with you
in the battles no one sees.

"Your Father, who sees what is done in secret, will reward you." — Matthew 6:6

Daily Challenge: Win a private battle today—choose obedience even when no one is watching.

Warrior's Prayer:
Father, strengthen me for the silent battles. Give me integrity that does not need an audience. Remind me that You see it all, and You reward what is done in the secret place. I fight for You alone. In Jesus' name, Amen.

July 9

"One touch of God's favor is worth a lifetime of labor."
Unknown

Son,

I can flip the battle in a heartbeat. I can part the sea at the last possible second. I can raise dry bones with a single breath. You think it's over—I'm just getting started.

Worry robs you of strength that belongs to faith. Anxiety clouds the victory that is already marching toward you. Stop rehearsing your fears. Start declaring My faithfulness. Trust that even if the story feels broken now, I am the Author—and I haven't finished writing.

I'm still on the throne. I'm still in the fire with you. And I will turn it for your good.

"At the proper time we will reap a harvest if we do not give up." — Galatians 6:9

Daily Challenge: Every time you feel anxiety today, immediately replace it with a declaration of God's promises.

Warrior's Prayer:
Father, teach me to trust Your timing more than my emotions. Remind me that You can change everything in a moment. I will not worry—I will worship while I wait. In Jesus' name, Amen.

July 10
"Delayed obedience is disobedience."
Charles Stanley

Son,
you think you're stuck waiting for a sign, for a miracle, for a breakthrough. But many times, I am waiting on you—to believe enough to move. To trust enough to act. To step even when the ground still looks unstable.

Faith doesn't sit and wait for perfect conditions. Faith moves based on My voice alone. Take the step, son. Trust that I will meet you there. Miracles often chase motion. Destiny often follows obedience. I will open doors—but first, you must walk to them.

Move, son. Faith was never meant to sit still.

"We live by faith, not by sight." — 2 Corinthians 5:7

Daily Challenge: Take one step of faith today, even if it feels risky or uncomfortable.

Warrior's Prayer:
Father, I refuse to let fear paralyze me. Strengthen my faith to step into the unknown, trusting You to catch me if I fall or carry me if I can't walk. I move today because You are faithful. In Jesus' name, Amen.

July 11

*"We are products of our past, but we don't
have to be prisoners of it."*
Rick Warren

Son,
the past is a battlefield I already conquered. You keep reaching back for chains I broke long ago. I didn't die for you to live shackled to regret. I didn't rise so you could stay buried in shame.

Your past has a place: beneath My feet. It has no right to define you. It has no authority to imprison you. I'm calling you forward, not backward. Let go of what I've already forgiven. Lay down what I've already redeemed. Your future is too bright for you to keep dragging dead weight. Walk free, son. Run free.

"Forget the former things; do not dwell on the past. See, I am doing a new thing!" — Isaiah 43:18–19

Daily Challenge: Today, speak out loud: "My past is under the blood. I will not carry what Christ already conquered."

Warrior's Prayer:
Father, thank You for defeating my past. I refuse to live chained to shame, guilt, or regret. Teach me to run forward with eyes fixed on You and hands free for battle. In Jesus' name, Amen.

July 12
"God is not looking for ability, but availability."
Hudson Taylor

Son,

I'm not searching for the strongest, fastest, or smartest—I'm searching for the willing. The world celebrates talent. I anoint surrender. I move mountains with mustard seeds of faith, not with resumes of perfection.

You don't have to impress Me to be used by Me. You just have to be available. Willing to go when others stay. Willing to speak when others stay silent. Willing to move when it feels risky. I can do more with one surrendered heart than an army of the proud. Open your hands, son. I will fill them with fire.

"Here am I. Send me!" — Isaiah 6:8

Daily Challenge: Tell God today: "Whatever You want, wherever You lead—I am available."

Warrior's Prayer:
Father, I give You my yes before I even know the question. Make me ready. Make me willing. Use my life for Your Kingdom no matter the cost. In Jesus' name, Amen.

July 13

"You may be weak, but God is strong – and His strength is made perfect in your weakness."
Charles Spurgeon

Son,
you don't discover strength
on the sidelines.

You discover it
when the battle leaves you breathless,
when the weight crushes your chest,
when you stand alone
and still refuse to fall.

Strength is not born in comfort.
It is revealed
when survival demands surrender to Me.

You are stronger than you feel
because I am stronger than your fear.

Stand, son.
Strength is already in your bones.

"The Lord is my strength and my shield; my heart trusts in Him, and He helps me." — Psalm 28:7

Daily Challenge: Face one fear head-on today—and remind yourself: "Strength is already inside me through Christ."

Warrior's Prayer:
Father, awaken the strength You have planted deep within me. When fear tries to paralyze me, let faith move my feet. I trust You for the power to stand, fight, and win. In Jesus' name, Amen.

July 14
"What you tolerate will eventually dominate."
Leonard Ravenhill

Son,
the enemy you ignore today becomes the giant you face tomorrow. I'm calling you to courage, not comfort. Victory doesn't come to those who avoid the fight—it comes to those who charge it.

You don't need to be fearless to fight—you just need to be faithful. I will be with you in the confrontation. I will fight alongside you. But you must step onto the battlefield. Face the fear. Face the wound. Face the habit. Face the lie. The sooner you confront it, the faster you conquer it.

Cowardice delays battles. Courage wins them.

"Be strong and courageous. Do not be afraid; do not be discouraged, for the Lord your God will be with you wherever you go." — Joshua 1:9

Daily Challenge: Identify one thing you've been avoiding—and today, confront it with prayer and action.

Warrior's Prayer:
Father, give me the courage to face what I fear. I will not hide from the fight You've equipped me to win. Strengthen my heart, sharpen my spirit, and lead me into victory. In Jesus' name, Amen.

July 15

*"I learned that courage was not the absence of fear,
but the triumph over it."*
Nelson Mandela

Son,
fear will always whisper in the darkness, but faith must roar in the light. Fear wants you small, silent, stuck. Faith demands you rise, speak, and move.

Fear says, "What if you fail?" Faith says, "What if God moves?" Fear says, "You're not enough." Faith says, "Christ is more than enough." The volume you listen to determines the direction you walk. Tune your ears to My promises, not your problems. Let faith roar louder than every lie.

You weren't built for timidity, son. You were forged for boldness.

"The righteous are as bold as a lion." — Proverbs 28:1

Daily Challenge: Speak faith out loud today whenever fear tries to rise.

Warrior's Prayer:
Father, let faith roar louder than fear inside me. Fill my heart with boldness that reflects Your strength. I will not live silent when You have called me to roar. In Jesus' name, Amen.

July 16

*"There is no panic in Heaven! God has
no problems, only plans."*
Corrie ten Boom

Son,
*sometimes you wonder where I am when the nights get long,
when the battle drags on, when your prayers seem
unanswered. But listen closely: I have not left you. I have not
gone silent. I am not ignoring you.*

*My patience is not My absence. I am working in dimensions
you can't see yet. I am aligning hearts, opening doors,
forging your spirit into something that can carry the weight
of what's coming. If I rushed the process, it would crush you.
But because I love you, I strengthen you first.*

*You are not abandoned—you are being anchored. You are
not forgotten—you are being fortified. When you can't see
My hand, trust My heart. My silence is not a no. It's a
preparation. And when the time is right, you'll see how every
moment of waiting was woven with My faithfulness.*

**"The Lord is not slow in keeping His promise, as some
understand slowness. Instead He is patient with you..."**
— 2 Peter 3:9

Daily Challenge: Resist the urge to rush God today. Choose to thank Him for the unseen work He's doing right now.

Warrior's Prayer:
Father, strengthen me in the waiting. When silence stretches long, remind me You are still near, still working, still reigning. Grow my trust deeper than my understanding. I will hold the line in faith until You call me forward. In Jesus' name, Amen.

July 17
"The cost of obedience is small compared with the cost of disobedience."
A.W. Tozer

Son,

comfort is not your goal—calling is. The world will lure you to stay safe, to seek ease, to blend in and avoid the fire. But I didn't call you to comfort. I called you to conquest. To mission. To movement.

Anointing doesn't fall on those who settle. It falls on those who surrender. Men who lay down their dreams for My dreams. Warriors who let Me break them and remake them. Champions who don't chase applause but chase obedience. You were never designed to live small. You were forged to carry My glory into dark places.

But to carry it, you must let go of the idols of comfort. You must be willing to be stretched, to bleed, to burn brighter. I am not looking for casual Christians. I am raising up fierce sons. You are one of them, son. Step into your calling. I will cover you with fire.

"But you are a chosen people, a royal priesthood, a holy nation, God's special possession..." — 1 Peter 2:9

Daily Challenge: Take one uncomfortable step toward obedience today—and thank God for stretching you.

Warrior's Prayer:
Father, destroy every comfort that keeps me from my calling. Anoint me to walk in places where fear cannot follow. Fill me with a fire that refuses to settle. I want Your mission more than my comfort. In Jesus' name, Amen.

July 18
"When all else fails, faith stands."
Corrie ten Boom

Son,
you pray for calm seas.
I allow storms.

Not to destroy you—
but to reveal you.

The storm strips away
the surface.
It exposes the roots.
It shows you
where you've anchored your soul.

When the winds howl,
the true warriors stand.
When the darkness falls,
the true faith shines.

You are not abandoned in the storm.
You are being revealed in it.

I have not sent the storm to sink you.
I have sent it to strengthen you.

Hold fast, son.
Your faith was born for this.

"The rain came down, the streams rose, and the winds blew and beat against that house; yet it did not fall..."
— Matthew 7:25

Daily Challenge: When something stressful hits today, immediately respond with prayer instead of panic.

Warrior's Prayer:
Father, reveal the roots of my faith through every storm. Strengthen my anchor in You alone. Let my life be built on the Rock that no storm can shake. I trust You to use even the fiercest winds to grow my heart stronger. In Jesus' name, Amen.

July 19
"You are not fighting FOR victory—you are fighting FROM it."
Tony Evans

Son,

you are not a desperate man clawing for scraps of hope. You are a son of the King, standing on ground that's already been won by the blood of Christ. The battle you face today is not to earn victory—it's to enforce it.

You don't have to prove yourself worthy. I already declared you worthy. You don't have to fear defeat. I already declared you victorious. The cross didn't just buy forgiveness—it bought unshakable victory over every lie, every attack, every giant that dares to rise against you.

Walk like it, son. Fight like it. Pray like it. The enemy trembles not because of your strength but because of the authority stamped onto your soul by the blood of the Lamb. You are a victor—now fight like one.

"But thanks be to God! He gives us the victory through our Lord Jesus Christ." — 1 Corinthians 15:57

Daily Challenge: Every time doubt rises today, respond: "I'm fighting from victory, not for it."

Warrior's Prayer:
Father, anchor my heart in the finished work of Christ. Teach me to fight, pray, live, and lead from the victory already purchased for me. Strengthen my hands for battle and my heart for endurance. I stand today already crowned by Your grace. In Jesus' name, Amen.

July 20
"Temptations and trials are the gymnasium for the soul."
Oswald Chambers

Son,

loss is not always defeat. Sometimes it's training. The battles you think you're losing are often the ones building you into the warrior I need for the bigger wars ahead.

When the fight feels relentless and you don't see the fruit yet, don't believe the lie that you're failing. You are learning endurance. You are sharpening discernment. You are strengthening spiritual muscle memory for battles you haven't even seen yet.

The enemy wants you to see only the scoreboard. I want you to see the shaping. Losing a skirmish doesn't mean losing the war. Stand up, wipe the blood from your face, and march forward. You are not losing—you are learning.

"Consider it pure joy, my brothers and sisters, whenever you face trials of many kinds, because you know that the testing of your faith produces perseverance."
— James 1:2–3

Daily Challenge: Reflect today on one "loss" in your life—and ask God to show you what He taught you through it.

Warrior's Prayer:
Father, teach me to value the lessons hidden inside every loss. Grow me through every wound. Shape me through every struggle. Make me into a warrior who sees beyond the pain to the purpose. I trust Your training. In Jesus' name, Amen.

July 21

*"Never be afraid to trust an unknown
future to a known God."*
Corrie ten Boom

Son,

you are standing at the edge, looking out at a future you can't predict. Fear will whisper a thousand questions: What if I fall? What if I fail? What if I lose everything?

But I am the God who already stands at the finish line. I am not wondering how your story ends. I have already written the final chapter in victory. You don't have to see the path perfectly to walk it powerfully—you only need to trust the One who carved it through mountains and storms.

The unknown is not your enemy. Fear is. Faith crushes fear at the gate. Faith steps even when the map is still blank. You are not following a plan—you are following a Person. Trust Me, son. I hold the future and I hold you.

"For I know the plans I have for you," declares the Lord, "plans to prosper you and not to harm you, plans to give you hope and a future." — Jeremiah 29:11

Daily Challenge: When fear about the future rises today, replace it immediately with this declaration: "My God already stands at my finish line."

Warrior's Prayer:
Father, I will not fear the future because You are already in it. Strengthen my faith to move when I can't see the way clearly. I trust Your heart even when the road ahead is hidden. My life is safe in Your hands. In Jesus' name, Amen.

July 22
*"God is most glorified in us when we are
most satisfied in Him."*
John Piper

Son,

you were not created to find satisfaction in applause, success, relationships, or security. Every other well you drink from will leave you thirstier than before. Only in Me will your soul find its home.

I want your heart fully alive, not barely surviving. The more you seek Me as your treasure, the more unshakable your joy becomes. Circumstances will change. People will fail you. Seasons will shift. But if your satisfaction is rooted in Me, no storm will uproot your spirit.

Glorify Me by loving Me above everything. Shine brightest not when life is perfect—but when life is hard, and you are still fully, deeply, fiercely satisfied in Me.

"Whom have I in heaven but You? And earth has nothing I desire besides You." — Psalm 73:25

Daily Challenge: Take 10 minutes today and worship God simply for who He is—not for what He can give you.

Warrior's Prayer:
Father, You are my portion, my treasure, and my home. Teach me to find my deepest joy not in what I have but in who You are. Satisfy my soul in You so fully that nothing on earth can steal my joy. In Jesus' name, Amen.

July 23

"Courage is almost a contradiction in terms. It means a strong desire to live taking the form of a readiness to die."
G.K. Chesterton

Son,
the enemy cannot take you out before your mission is complete. Your life is not fragile when it is placed in My hands. You are not at the mercy of random chaos—you are held by sovereign design.

Walk boldly. Fear nothing. You are immortal in the center of My will until the day I call you home. I have assigned you to this generation, to this time, to these battles. And no enemy can erase what I have commissioned you to accomplish.

Do not tiptoe through life trying to avoid pain. Charge forward knowing that My purpose is your shield. As long as I have work for you, nothing—no sickness, no enemy, no setback—can stop you. Live like a man with Heaven's authority stamped on his chest.

"I shall not die, but I shall live, and recount the deeds of the Lord." — Psalm 118:17

Daily Challenge: Walk fearlessly today—remind yourself hourly: "I am immortal until God is finished with me."

Warrior's Prayer:
Father, thank You that my life is in Your hands, not the enemy's. Fill me with courage to live boldly, fight fiercely, and love deeply without fear. I will run this race without hesitation until the day You call me home. In Jesus' name, Amen.

July 24

*"Expect great things from God; attempt
great things for God."*
William Carey

*Son,
you expect too little
and attempt even less.*

*I am not a small God.
You were not made for small dreams.*

*Expect the impossible, son.
Attempt the miraculous.
Pray like Heaven listens.
Move like Heaven backs you.*

*You were not saved
to live safe.
You were not called
to live careful.*

*Dare to risk for My Kingdom.
Dare to fight when others run.
Dare to attempt what only faith can accomplish.*

*Great battles are waiting.
Great victories are promised.
Great things are born
in daring sons.*

"Now to Him who is able to do immeasurably more than all we ask or imagine..." — Ephesians 3:20

Daily Challenge: Attempt something bold for God today—even if it feels beyond your strength.

Warrior's Prayer:
Father, ignite courage inside me to expect and attempt great things for Your glory. Let my faith be bigger than my fear. I refuse to live small when You are calling me to live for the impossible. In Jesus' name, Amen.

July 25

*"He is no fool who gives what he cannot
keep to gain what he cannot lose."*
Jim Elliot

Son,
the world will tell you to clutch tightly to what fades—
money, fame, comfort, control. But I am telling you to let it
go. You cannot keep what this world offers. You were made
for a Kingdom that cannot be shaken.

Every sacrifice for My sake is a seed planted in eternity.
Every risk for My name is a crown forged in glory. Every act
of surrender is an investment that never rots, rusts, or fades
away. Don't live your life trading eternal treasures for
temporary toys.

Hold loosely what the world worships. Hold tightly to Me.
What you give to Me will never be lost. What you give up for
Me will be multiplied beyond imagination.

"Do not store up for yourselves treasures on earth... but store up for yourselves treasures in heaven."
— Matthew 6:19–20

Daily Challenge: Give something valuable today—your time, money, energy—for a cause that impacts eternity.

Warrior's Prayer:
Father, loosen my grip on everything temporary. Teach me to give generously, risk boldly, and surrender fully for Your glory. I will not waste my life chasing what cannot last. I want treasures that time and death cannot touch. In Jesus' name, Amen.

July 26
"When Christ calls a man, He bids him come and die."
Dietrich Bonhoeffer

Son,
I didn't call you to an easier life—I called you to a crucified one. Following Me isn't about polishing your image or chasing comfort. It's about laying down your pride, your preferences, your plans, and your fears.

I am calling you to die—die to selfishness, die to fear, die to living small. Because only the dead can truly live. Only those who surrender fully can be raised fully. Only those who lose their lives for My sake will find a life fiercer, fuller, freer than anything the world could ever offer.

Don't fear the death of your old self. Embrace it. Every nail driven into your flesh-driven dreams will be answered by resurrection power. Come and die, son—and rise with Me into unstoppable life.

"I have been crucified with Christ and I no longer live, but Christ lives in me." — Galatians 2:20

Daily Challenge: Today, ask yourself before every decision: "Am I living to please myself or to glorify Christ?"

Warrior's Prayer:
Father, I choose the cross over comfort. Crucify my pride, my fear, my selfish ambitions. Raise me up in the power of Christ's life. Teach me to lose my life for Your sake so that I might truly find it. In Jesus' name, Amen.

July 27
*"Faith is taking the first step even when you
don't see the whole staircase."*
Martin Luther King Jr.

Son,
I'm not asking you to see the whole journey. I'm asking you to trust the next step. Obedience rarely comes with a detailed map—it comes with a whispered call and a choice to move.

You want certainty, but I offer you Myself. You want control, but I offer you faith. The next step will not always make sense. It will not always feel safe. But it will always be significant. Each act of obedience builds a staircase into your destiny—one step, one stone, one sacrifice at a time.

Move, son. Even when you can't see the top. Especially when you can't see the top. I am waiting for you on every level.

"We walk by faith, not by sight." — 2 Corinthians 5:7

Daily Challenge: Take one step of faith today toward something God has put on your heart, even if it feels small or uncertain.

Warrior's Prayer:
Father, give me the courage to move even when I cannot see the whole way forward. Strengthen my steps with trust, not sight. Build my life into something greater than fear would allow. I trust Your voice more than I trust my eyes. In Jesus' name, Amen.

July 28

"God loves each of us as if there were only one of us."
St. Augustine

Son,
you are not lost
in a crowd of prayers.

You are not another face
in a sea of souls.

You are seen.
You are heard.
You are fiercely, intimately, relentlessly loved.

Not tolerated.
Not overlooked.
Loved.

I see the tremble in your hands.
I see the fire flickering in your chest.
I see the longing you barely admit aloud.

And I call you by name,
again and again and again.

You are My son.
And I love you
like you are My only son.

Because you are priceless to Me.

"I have loved you with an everlasting love; I have drawn you with unfailing kindness." — Jeremiah 31:3

Daily Challenge: Meditate today on the fact that God's love for you is deeply personal—write a short prayer or journal entry about it.

Warrior's Prayer:
Father, thank You for loving me not as one among many but as Your beloved son. Burn this truth into my bones. Let every decision I make flow from the security of Your unstoppable love. In Jesus' name, Amen.

July 29

"We are always preparing to live but never living."
Ralph Waldo Emerson

Son,
today is a seed.
Today is not just another day to survive—it's a day to prepare for what's coming. Victories are won not by wishful thinking, but by faithful planting.

The discipline you choose today fuels the destiny you walk into tomorrow. The small choices, the hidden prayers, the unseen sacrifices—they forge the man who will rise when the world shakes. Don't waste the day waiting for a better one. This day is the battlefield where tomorrow's victories are born.

Prepare your heart. Sharpen your sword. Build your endurance. Tomorrow belongs to the warriors who prepared in the quiet places when no one was watching.

"The plans of the diligent lead surely to abundance."
— Proverbs 21:5

Daily Challenge: Choose one area of your life where you need to prepare better—and take one deliberate action today toward it.

Warrior's Prayer:
Father, teach me the value of today's discipline. Let me not waste a moment You've given me. Strengthen my resolve to prepare, to sharpen, to stand ready for what You have called me to. In Jesus' name, Amen.

July 30
*"I am not afraid of storms, for I am
learning how to sail my ship."*
Louisa May Alcott

Son,

storms are not signals of failure—they are training grounds for greatness. Calm seas don't build captains. Smooth waters don't sharpen warriors. I send you into storms not to drown you, but to teach your hands the ropes and your heart the rhythms of My strength.

When the winds roar and the sails strain, that's when your faith is forged. That's when your leadership sharpens. That's when you learn to trust My whisper over the howling winds. Don't curse the storm. Learn in it. Rise in it. Let it make you the kind of man who can weather any future wave.

The storm is not here to stop you. It's here to strengthen you.

"Then they cried out to the Lord in their trouble, and He brought them out of their distress. He stilled the storm to a whisper." — Psalm 107:28–29

Daily Challenge: When you face pressure today, ask: "Father, what are You teaching me through this?"

Warrior's Prayer:
Father, I will not curse the storm. Teach my hands to steer and my heart to trust You more deeply. Build a warrior's endurance in me. Let every wave drive me closer to Your heart. In Jesus' name, Amen.

July 31

"The best use of life is love. The best expression of love is time. The best time to love is now."
Rick Warren

Son,
you think you have time.
You think love can wait.
You think the right moment will present itself later.

But later is not guaranteed.

Love while you can.
Forgive quickly.
Speak courage boldly.
Lay down your pride sacrificially.

You were not placed here to build monuments to yourself.
You were placed here to love well, fight for others, and leave a wake of hope behind you.

Don't waste your life chasing what rusts and rots.
Spend it. Pour it out.
Now.
While you still have breath.

"And now these three remain: faith, hope and love. But the greatest of these is love." — 1 Corinthians 13:13

Daily Challenge: Love intentionally today. Reach out to one person you've been meaning to encourage or forgive—and do it before the sun sets.

Warrior's Prayer:
Father, teach me to love like You love—fiercely, freely, fully. Let me not wait until it's convenient. Let me spend my life pouring hope, courage, and mercy into others for Your glory. I will not delay what matters most. In Jesus' name, Amen.

August 1

"The measure of a man's greatness is not the number of servants he has, but the number of people he serves."
John C. Maxwell

Son,

greatness in My Kingdom is upside-down from the world's view. They chase titles; I call you to carry towels. They race for recognition; I send you to the hidden places where service is unseen but eternal.

You become great not by climbing over others, but by kneeling beneath them. Every time you choose to serve instead of demand, to lift instead of lord over, you reflect the heart of My Son. The cross was not forced upon Him—He carried it by choice, in love.

You want to lead well? Serve well first. The weight of My Kingdom rests on the shoulders of those who kneel.

"Whoever wants to become great among you must be your servant." — Matthew 20:26

Daily Challenge: Find one way today to serve someone sacrificially without expecting anything in return.

Warrior's Prayer:
Father, teach me the greatness of humility. Make me a man who carries towels, not titles. Shape my heart to find joy in serving when no one notices but You. I want to reflect the heart of Christ today. In Jesus' name, Amen.

August 2
*"This is the day that the Lord has made;
let us rejoice and be glad in it."*
Psalm 118:24

Son,
I created you not to simply exist but to live—fully, fearlessly, joyfully. Too many live small because fear has convinced them that it's safer to shrink than to stretch. But I call you to love this life I've breathed into you. I call you to embrace each moment with gratitude and purpose.

When you see life as a gift, it becomes a weapon against despair. When you live from a posture of thankfulness, even your darkest days are laced with light. Love the life I've given you, son. Not because it's perfect, but because it's a battleground worth fighting for.

The enemy comes to steal, kill, and destroy. I came to give you life—abundant, relentless, victorious.

> **"I have come that they may have life, and have it to the full."** — John 10:10

Daily Challenge: Speak life today—every conversation, every action, infuse it with gratitude and joy.

Warrior's Prayer:
Father, thank You for the gift of life. Teach me to love fiercely, to live fully, and to fight for joy even when battles rage. Let my life be a bright defiance against darkness. In Jesus' name, Amen.

August 3

"The prayer that prevails is not the one that rambles but the one that pierces heaven."
Charles Spurgeon

Son,
your prayers don't need to be long—they need to be alive. I'm not impressed by empty phrases. I'm moved by fierce, honest, desperate cries of faith.

The prayers that shake earth and open Heaven are the ones soaked in fire, fueled by surrender, marked by boldness. Come to Me not with rehearsed lines but with a warrior's cry. I do not ignore My sons when they pray with hearts stripped of performance and filled with holy hunger.

Pray like the battlefield depends on it—because it does. Heaven moves when My sons roar in faith.

"The prayer of a righteous person is powerful and effective." — James 5:16

Daily Challenge: Spend time today praying with raw honesty—drop the script and pour your heart out boldly to God.

Warrior's Prayer:
Father, ignite my prayers with fire today. Teach me to pray not to impress but to invade the darkness. Let my words pierce the heavens and pull down Your Kingdom into this battle-scarred world. I am not here to whisper—I am here to roar. In Jesus' name, Amen.

August 4

"My main ambition in life is to be on the devil's most wanted list."
Leonard Ravenhil

Son,
half-hearted warriors
lose whole battles.

Lukewarm hearts
build no Kingdoms.
Casual faith
wins no wars.

Give Me everything.

Hold nothing back.
No secret fears.
No private idols.
No halfway prayers.

A life fully surrendered
is a torch in My hand.

A man fully consecrated
shakes nations,
splits darkness,
awakens generations.

Don't live half-alive, son.
Burn.
Fully.
Forever.
For Me.

"Love the Lord your God with all your heart and with all your soul and with all your mind and with all your strength." — Mark 12:30

Daily Challenge: Today, identify one area of your life you're still holding back from God and surrender it fully.

Warrior's Prayer:
Father, consume every part of my life. Burn away the hesitation, the idols, the half-measures. Make me fully, dangerously, gloriously Yours. Let my life set fires of faith wherever You send me. In Jesus' name, Amen.

August 5
"Courage is not the absence of fear, but the triumph over it."
Nelson Mandela

Son,

fear will always whisper. Courage isn't about never hearing fear—it's about refusing to obey it. Every warrior you admire faced trembling hands and pounding hearts. The difference was they stood anyway.

Victory does not belong to those who feel the safest. It belongs to those who move forward when fear snarls at their feet. You are not called to feel brave. You are called to act brave. And I have not given you a spirit of fear, but of power, love, and a sound mind.

Fear may roar, but My Spirit roars louder within you.

"Be strong and courageous. Do not be afraid; do not be discouraged, for the Lord your God will be with you wherever you go." — Joshua 1:9

Daily Challenge: Do something courageous today—something that scares you but honors God.

Warrior's Prayer:
Father, fill me with holy courage. When fear whispers defeat, let Your voice thunder victory. Strengthen my hands, steady my heart, and set my spirit ablaze to do hard things for Your glory. In Jesus' name, Amen.

August 6

"We are all faced with a series of great opportunities brilliantly disguised as impossible situations."
Charles R. Swindoll

Son,
the battlefield often looks like chaos before it looks like victory. The greatest opportunities I place in your life won't come gift-wrapped—they'll come wrapped in impossibility.

What looks overwhelming to you is already orchestrated by My hand. Giants fall to stones. Seas part with staffs. Prisons open with praise. Stop seeing impossibility as a stop sign. Start seeing it as an invitation. I do My best work when you step into the fight believing not in your strength, but in Mine.

You were never meant to live small, cautious, or afraid. I made you to storm walls, to slay giants, to take ground. Every impossible situation is simply a miracle waiting for your obedience.

"With man this is impossible, but with God all things are possible." — Matthew 19:26

Daily Challenge: Face one "impossible" thing today head-on—and invite God to work through it.

Warrior's Prayer:
Father, train my eyes to see opportunities where others see impossibility. Give me courage to step into the unknown, trusting Your power more than my limitations. I believe You for miracles today. In Jesus' name, Amen.

August 7
"Do small things with great love."
Mother Teresa

Son,

greatness isn't always found in grand gestures. Sometimes it's hidden in the smallest acts—the quiet sacrifices no one sees, the tiny seeds of kindness planted in hard soil.

You want to do big things for Me? Start small, but start with great love. Every small prayer, every hidden act of service, every unnoticed gift of encouragement—it matters. I see it. I multiply it. I weave it into the fabric of eternity.

You are not wasting your strength when you serve quietly. You are wielding a sword sharper than the applause of men. Serve where you are. Love where you are. Plant seeds today that will shake generations tomorrow.

"Whatever you did for one of the least of these brothers and sisters of Mine, you did for Me." — Matthew 25:40

Daily Challenge: Choose one small act of love today for someone who cannot repay you—and do it quietly.

Warrior's Prayer:
Father, teach me to love in the small things. Grow a heart in me that sees every person, every moment, every opportunity as sacred. Let my life be a river of Your kindness, flowing into a world desperate for hope. In Jesus' name, Amen.

August 8

"Our greatest fear should not be of failure, but of succeeding at things in life that don't really matter."
Francis Chan

Son,
you were not made
to build sandcastles on shores
that eternity will wash away.

You were not made
to chase crowns that rust,
or applause that fades.

Measure your victories, son,
not by the size of the stage,
but by the weight of their worth in Heaven.

Succeed in surrender.
Conquer in obedience.
Win in love.

Succeed where it matters—
in souls saved,
in battles fought for My name,
in legacies that echo in eternity.

"What good will it be for someone to gain the whole world, yet forfeit their soul?" — Matthew 16:26

Daily Challenge: Take inventory today: Are you spending your energy on things that matter for eternity—or just for today?

Warrior's Prayer:
Father, align my heart with what truly matters. Strip away every empty pursuit. Teach me to live for what echoes in Heaven, not what fades on earth. I want to succeed only where You say it counts. In Jesus' name, Amen.

August 9

*"Anxiety does not empty tomorrow of its sorrows,
but only empties today of its strength."*
Charles Spurgeon

Son,
anxiety is a thief. It robs you of peace, of focus, of strength you need for today. Worry about tomorrow will never change tomorrow—it will only weaken today.

You cannot control the future. You are not meant to carry it. I hold tomorrow in My hands. Your only job is to be faithful with today—to love deeply, fight bravely, pray fiercely, and trust relentlessly.

When fear whispers about tomorrow, shout My promises louder. When anxiety rises, crush it under the weight of My sovereignty. You were not built to be weighed down by what hasn't even happened yet.

Lift your eyes. Breathe deep. Today has enough battles of its own—and I will supply everything you need to win them.

"Therefore do not worry about tomorrow, for tomorrow will worry about itself. Each day has enough trouble of its own." — Matthew 6:34

Daily Challenge: Every time a fearful thought about the future enters your mind today, crush it immediately with a Scripture promise.

Warrior's Prayer:
Father, teach me to fight the battles of today with a full heart and an unburdened mind. I cast every future fear into Your faithful hands. Give me strength for this day and trust for every day to come. In Jesus' name, Amen.

August 10

*"It is not the strength of the body that counts,
but the strength of the spirit."*
J.R.R. Tolkien

Son,
the world trains bodies for battle. I train spirits for victory. Muscle will fail. Charm will fade. Wealth will crumble. But a spirit forged in My fire—that spirit endures storms and shakes kingdoms.

You do not conquer by flesh. You conquer by faith. You do not outlast enemies by your willpower but by My Spirit pulsing inside your bones. Strength is not found in the arm that swings the sword, but in the heart that refuses to lay it down.

Feed your spirit more fiercely than you feed your fears. Build an inner fortress with My Word, My promises, My presence. This is how true warriors rise.

"Not by might nor by power, but by My Spirit," says the Lord Almighty." — Zechariah 4:6

Daily Challenge: Do one thing today to intentionally strengthen your spirit—whether prayer, Scripture memory, or fasting.

Warrior's Prayer:
Father, build a spirit inside me that the world cannot crush. Strengthen my inner man until he outlasts every battle, every betrayal, every storm. Teach me to draw power from Your Spirit, not from my own limited strength. In Jesus' name, Amen.

August 11
*"We are too busy to pray, and so we are
too busy to have power."*
E.M. Bounds

Son,
busyness is one of the enemy's most subtle weapons. If he can't make you fall, he'll try to make you frantic. If he can't stop you with fear, he'll smother you with distractions. You don't lose power because you're attacked—you lose power when you disconnect from Me.

Prayer is not a duty to check off your list. It is the oxygen your spirit breathes. It is the fuel that sets your steps ablaze with purpose. It is your battle cry, your fortress, your lifeline. Without it, you are only surviving. With it, you are unstoppable.

Don't let the urgent push out the essential. Drop everything before you drop prayer. I have victories waiting for you—but you must be plugged into My power to walk them out.

"Pray without ceasing." — 1 Thessalonians 5:17

Daily Challenge: Block out a set, protected time today to pray with no phone, no noise, no distractions. Guard it like a warrior.

Warrior's Prayer:
Father, forgive me for letting busyness drown out intimacy. Call me back to the battlefield of prayer. Fill me with a hunger for Your presence stronger than any distraction. Teach me to draw strength from time at Your feet. In Jesus' name, Amen.

August 12

*"You can give without loving, but you
cannot love without giving."*
Amy Carmichael

Son,
love that costs nothing accomplishes nothing. True love moves. True love sacrifices. True love gives—time, energy, resources, forgiveness, compassion—without demanding anything in return.

I didn't just love you with words—I loved you with wounds. I didn't just speak My affection—I nailed it to a cross. If you want to walk as My son, you must love like My Son: fiercely, sacrificially, relentlessly.

Loving when it's easy changes nothing. Loving when it hurts shakes hell. This is the battleground where sons become warriors. Give where it costs you. Love where it stretches you. This is how the world will see Me in you.

"Greater love has no one than this: to lay down one's life for one's friends." — John 15:13

Daily Challenge: Choose to give sacrificially today—your time, your forgiveness, your energy—to someone who needs it most.

Warrior's Prayer:
Father, make my love active, costly, and real. Break the chains of selfishness and fill me with the courage to love like You loved me. Let my life be a reflection of Your fierce, sacrificial heart. In Jesus' name, Amen.

August 13
"The Bible is not an option; it is a necessity."
Billy Graham

Son,

you are fighting a war you cannot see. Every day lies try to drown out the truth. Every moment, temptation tries to rewrite your identity. If you fight without a sword, you will fall. If you run without armor, you will bleed.

My Word is your weapon. It is not a dusty book for the weak—it is a living sword for the strong. When you wield My promises, darkness retreats. When you sharpen your mind with My truth, deception crumbles. A man who carries Scripture in his bones will not be easily broken.

Don't treat My Word like an accessory. Treat it like a lifeline. Read it. Memorize it. Speak it aloud over your battles. The greatest warriors are those whose swords never leave their sides.

"For the word of God is alive and active. Sharper than any double-edged sword..." — Hebrews 4:12

Daily Challenge: Spend intentional time today memorizing a new verse—and declare it aloud when you face opposition.

Warrior's Prayer:
Father, embed Your Word deep into my heart. Make it the first weapon I reach for when the battle rages. Teach my hands to wield Scripture like a sword and my heart to trust it like a shield. In Jesus' name, Amen.

August 14

"What you do in the secret place will show in the public place." Paul Washer

Son,
private battles
build public victories.

What you win
when no one sees
determines how you stand
when the world watches.

Pray in secret.
Fight in secret.
Surrender in secret.

Let the hidden places
become holy ground.

Let the unseen hours
forge an unshakable man.

You were not made
for performances.
You were made
for perseverance.

The secret place
is where kings are crowned
and warriors are born.

"Then your Father, who sees what is done in secret, will reward you." — Matthew 6:6

Daily Challenge: Carve out hidden time with God today no posting about it, no announcing it. Just you and Him.

Warrior's Prayer:
Father, teach me the power of the secret place. Build in me a life of unseen victories that explode into public faithfulness. Let my foundation be deep, fierce, and invisible to the world—but unshakable before You. In Jesus' name, Amen.

August 15
*"You will never change your life until you
change something you do daily."*
John C. Maxwell

Son,
*destiny is not built in one bold leap—it is forged in a
thousand small decisions. The habits you form today are the
bricks you lay for tomorrow's battles, victories, and
legacies.*

*You want to change your life? Change your patterns. Anchor
yourself daily in prayer. Sharpen yourself daily in My Word.
Strengthen yourself daily in discipline. What you do daily
will either become your downfall or your deliverance.*

*Stop waiting for inspiration. Start building with intention.
Tiny hinges swing mighty doors. Small seeds bring massive
harvests. Faithfulness today unlocks favor tomorrow.*

**"Whoever can be trusted with very little can also be
trusted with much."** — Luke 16:10

Daily Challenge: Start (or reinforce) one daily habit today
that builds your spirit—prayer, Scripture, discipline—and
commit to it for 30 days.

Warrior's Prayer:
Father, teach me the power of small, faithful steps. Help me
to build daily rhythms of obedience and strength that carry
me through every battle ahead. Let my life be marked by
hidden faithfulness that bears visible fruit. In Jesus' name,
Amen.

August 16
"When I am weak, then I am strong."
The Apostle Paul (2 Corinthians 12:10)

Son,
you've been trained to hide your weakness, to mask your scars, to flex strength even when you're breaking inside. But My Kingdom works differently. In the world, weakness disqualifies. In My Kingdom, weakness invites supernatural strength.

You don't have to be enough. You were never meant to be. I am your enough. When you reach the end of yourself—when the muscles fail, when the strategies crumble, when the pride dies—that's when My power roars into your life.

You don't need to impress Me with toughness. You need to trust Me with surrender. When you admit your need, you unleash My fullness. Let the world see a man unashamed of his weakness because he is filled with the strength of an unshakable God.

"But He said to me, 'My grace is sufficient for you, for My power is made perfect in weakness.'"
— 2 Corinthians 12:9

Daily Challenge: Identify one weakness you usually hide—and today, invite God's strength into it through prayer.

Warrior's Prayer:
Father, I am done pretending to be strong without You. I lay my weakness at Your feet and ask for Your power to flood my heart. Teach me that surrender is the gateway to victory. In Jesus' name, Amen.

August 17

"There is no pit so deep that God's love is not deeper still."
— Corrie ten Boom

Son,

sometimes the darkness feels endless. Sometimes the pit feels too deep, the shame too thick, the defeat too permanent. But listen: there is no depth to which My love cannot reach.

No sin, no failure, no betrayal can outrun My mercy. I have descended into the lowest hells of human pain and crushed them under My feet. When you cry out from the pit, My hand is already reaching down to pull you out. There is no height or depth, no demon or disaster that can separate you from Me.

You are not forgotten in the dark. You are found by a love that digs deeper than despair. Hold on, son. I have you—and I will never let go.

"For I am convinced that neither death nor life, neither angels nor demons... will be able to separate us from the love of God." — Romans 8:38–39

Daily Challenge: When discouragement whispers today, shout back: "God's love goes deeper than this."

Warrior's Prayer:
Father, when I feel like the pit is too deep, remind me that Your arms reach further still. Pull me up by Your mercy. Surround me with a love that darkness cannot diminish. I trust You to rescue and restore. In Jesus' name, Amen.

August 18

"You cannot swim for new horizons until you have courage to lose sight of the shore."
William Faulkner

Son,
the shore feels safe
because it is familiar.

But I have called you
to deeper waters.

You cannot walk on water
while clinging to the sand.

You cannot conquer new territory
while staring backward at comfort.

Let go, son.
Let the waves carry you
where faith is the only map.

I am the horizon
you cannot yet see—
but I am already there,
waiting for you.

Leave the shore.
Come walk on waves.

"Immediately Jesus made the disciples get into the boat and go on ahead of Him to the other side..."
— Matthew 14:22

Daily Challenge: Take one step today into something unknown where you must fully trust God's leadership.

Warrior's Prayer:
Father, give me the courage to leave the familiar behind. Lead me into deeper waters where my faith has no safety nets but Your voice alone. Strengthen my spirit to trust You even when the shore disappears. In Jesus' name, Amen.

August 19

"Faith sees the invisible, believes the unbelievable, and receives the impossible."
Corrie ten Boom

Son,

faith isn't anchored in what you see—it's anchored in Who you trust. Sight walks by facts. Faith walks by promises. And when you walk by faith, you access a dimension where miracles are normal and impossibilities are just invitations.

I am calling you to be a man who sees what others cannot, believes what others laugh at, and walks where others refuse to tread. You were not created for a predictable life—you were created for a life that makes no sense apart from the power of God.

Don't shrink your prayers to fit your sight. Expand your faith to match My size. Dream beyond the visible. Believe beyond the believable. Expect the impossible.

"Now faith is confidence in what we hope for and assurance about what we do not see."
— Hebrews 11:1

Daily Challenge: Today, pray for something bigger than you can accomplish alone—something that only God can do.

Warrior's Prayer:
Father, increase my faith until it terrifies fear. Teach me to see with Heaven's eyes, believe with Heaven's heart, and move with Heaven's courage. I refuse to live a life explainable without You. In Jesus' name, Amen.

August 20
"We are not called to be successful. We are called to be faithful."
Mother Teresa

Son,
the world worships results. I celebrate faithfulness. Success can be stripped away by storms, by betrayal, by circumstances outside your control. But faithfulness—faithfulness crowns you with eternal victory that no man, no demon, no disaster can steal.

You don't have to outshine others. You have to outlast the lies. You don't have to be applauded. You have to be anchored. I measure greatness not by how far you climb but by how fiercely you stay faithful when the crowds disappear.

Run your race, son. Run it steady. Run it faithful. Leave the scoreboard to Me.

"Well done, good and faithful servant!"
— Matthew 25:23

Daily Challenge: Focus today not on results—but on being radically faithful in one small thing God has called you to do.

Warrior's Prayer:
Father, shift my heart from chasing success to chasing You. Anchor me in faithfulness even when the rewards are invisible. Teach me that finishing well is better than starting fast. I run for Your applause alone. In Jesus' name, Amen.

August 21

"God never said the journey would be easy, but He did say the arrival would be worthwhile."
Max Lucado

Son,
the road I have called you to walk is not paved with ease. It is forged through fire, sharpened by storms, carved by sacrifice. There will be days you limp. There will be nights you question. There will be seasons you feel like crawling when you used to run.

But hear Me clearly: every step matters. Every scar has meaning. Every setback will be woven into a greater victory you cannot yet see. I am not wasting your pain. I am not overlooking your tears. I am preparing a future for you that will make every battle, every bruise, every broken dream worth it.

The journey is hard. But the arrival—the moment you step across the finish line into My arms—will be breathtaking.

"I consider that our present sufferings are not worth comparing with the glory that will be revealed in us."
— Romans 8:18

Daily Challenge: Endure today with this mindset: "My journey is hard, but my destination is glorious."

Warrior's Prayer:
Father, when the road is long, lift my head. When the battle wears me down, strengthen my spirit. Remind me daily that the finish line is worth every tear and every step. I run for Your glory alone. In Jesus' name, Amen.

August 22

*"True humility is not thinking less of yourself;
it is thinking of yourself less."*
C.S. Lewis

Son,
pride whispers you are the center of the story. But the real battle is won when you step out of the spotlight and into servanthood. True humility isn't weakness—it's the fierce, powerful strength to lift others higher without needing to be seen.

The most dangerous men in My Kingdom are not the ones who demand recognition—they are the ones who quietly fight for others, who lay down their rights, who use their strength to shield the weak.

Live with your eyes off yourself, son. See the wounded. Hear the cries. Build up those around you. When you choose humility, I raise you higher than pride ever could.

"Humble yourselves, therefore, under God's mighty hand, that He may lift you up in due time." — 1 Peter 5:6

Daily Challenge: Serve someone today in a way that costs you comfort—and do it without needing acknowledgment.

Warrior's Prayer:
Father, kill the pride in me that demands attention. Shape my heart to live for You and others, not for applause. Teach me the strength of humility and the power of selfless service. In Jesus' name, Amen.

August 23

*"You are never too old to set another goal
or to dream a new dream."*
C.S. Lewis

Son,
you think it's too late.
You think you missed it.
You think the dream is dead.

It's not.

Dreams don't die
when I am the Author.
Visions don't expire
when I am the Breath behind them.

I do not measure by clocks,
by calendars,
by the regrets of yesterday.

New dreams
can be born in old hearts.
New fires
can blaze from the ashes of past failures.

If you still have breath,
you still have purpose.
If you still have desire,
you still have destiny.

Dream again, son.
Set your eyes higher.
Plant your feet deeper.
We are just getting started.

"Forget the former things; do not dwell on the past. See, I am doing a new thing!" — Isaiah 43:18–19

Daily Challenge: Pray boldly today: "Father, resurrect every God-given dream inside me that fear has tried to bury."

Warrior's Prayer:
Father, breathe new dreams into me today. Awaken dead hopes. Ignite dormant callings. Remind me that age, failure, or fear cannot stop what You have ordained. I choose to dream again with You. In Jesus' name, Amen.

August 24

"Success is on the same road as failure; success is just a little further down the road."
Jack Hyles

Son,
failure is not a dead end—it's a crossroads. Too many stop when they stumble, thinking they've been disqualified. But My sons? They rise. They wipe the blood from their knuckles and keep walking.

The enemy would love nothing more than for you to mistake a momentary defeat for a permanent destiny. But I use every fall to teach, to refine, to sharpen. Every setback is preparation. Every failure is fuel. Success isn't found by avoiding the fall—it's found by refusing to quit after it.

Stay the course. Push through the breaking points. Success isn't some distant, unreachable place—it's just a few more faithful steps down the road.

"Though the righteous fall seven times, they rise again."
— Proverbs 24:16

Daily Challenge: Identify an area where you've been tempted to give up—and today, recommit to pressing forward.

Warrior's Prayer:
Father, strengthen my spirit to endure beyond failure. When I fall, lift my eyes. When I stumble, steady my feet. Teach me to see defeat not as my grave but as my training ground. I will not quit. I will rise. In Jesus' name, Amen.

August 25

*"He who has God and everything else has no
more than he who has God only."*
C.S. Lewis

*Son,
you chase many things—
success, security, approval, comfort.
But in the end,
only one thing matters.*

Me.

*When you have Me,
you lack nothing.
When you lose everything
but still have Me,
you have lost nothing.*

*Everything else
is smoke.
Shadows.
Temporary victories
and fading crowns.*

*I am your prize.
I am your portion.
I am your final victory.
When the world crumbles,
I remain.
When kingdoms fall,
I stand.*

Anchor your heart in Me, son.

"The Lord is my portion," says my soul, "therefore I will hope in Him." — Lamentations 3:24

Daily Challenge: Spend time today thanking God for who He is—*not* for what He gives.

Warrior's Prayer:
Father, You are enough for me. Strip away every false treasure that competes for my heart. Teach me to anchor my hope not in blessings but in the Blesser Himself. I will seek You above all else. In Jesus' name, Amen.

August 26
"When you can't trace His hand, trust His heart."
Charles Spurgeon

Son,
there will be days you cannot see what I'm doing.
You'll stand at the edge of decisions, battles, storms—
and it will feel like My hand is hidden.
But hear Me clearly:
My heart for you is never hidden.

When the path is dark, trust My character.
When the answers don't come, trust My promises.
When the breakthrough feels delayed, trust My timing.
I have not abandoned you in the fog—I am closer than your breath.

You don't have to understand everything to obey.
You don't have to feel everything to believe.
You have My heart, son—fierce, faithful, forever yours.

"Trust in the Lord with all your heart and lean not on your own understanding." — Proverbs 3:5

Daily Challenge: Choose trust over control today in one area where you're tempted to doubt God's goodness.

Warrior's Prayer:
Father, when I can't trace Your hand, teach me to trust Your heart. Strengthen my spirit to obey without full understanding. Let my trust in You be stronger than my need to know everything. In Jesus' name, Amen.

August 27
"Only a real risk tests the reality of a belief."
C.S. Lewis

Son,
safe faith is not real faith.
Real faith looks like stepping out while your knees shake.
It looks like building an ark when there's no rain,
like marching around walls before they fall,
like charging Goliath with just a sling and a shout.

Faith isn't faith until it risks something—your reputation, your comfort, your logic.
You cannot live dangerously for My Kingdom and safely for yourself at the same time.

The world doesn't need more cautious believers.
It needs dangerous warriors who trust Me enough to risk big.
I will meet you in the risk, son. I always have.

"Without faith it is impossible to please God..." —
Hebrews 11:6

Daily Challenge: Take one bold step of risk today for God's glory—something that stretches your faith.

Warrior's Prayer:
Father, ignite daring faith inside me. Break the chains of fear, pride, and self-preservation. Teach me to step onto battlefields that feel too big because You are bigger still. I want to live dangerously for Your name. In Jesus' name, Amen.

August 28

*"There is no greater agony than bearing an
untold story inside you."*
Maya Angelou

Son,
there is a story inside you
that hell is terrified of.

A story of scars that became swords.
Of weakness that became worship.
Of fear that became fire.

The enemy wants you silent,
ashamed,
afraid.

But I am calling you
to speak.

Your story is not a shame to hide.
It is a weapon to wield.
It is a light for the broken,
a banner for the weary,
a battle cry for the forgotten.

Tell it, son.
Tell it even if your voice trembles.
Tell it because someone's freedom
is waiting on your courage.

"Let the redeemed of the Lord tell their story."
— Psalm 107:2

Daily Challenge: Share one part of your testimony today with someone who needs hope.

Warrior's Prayer:

Father, give me courage to tell the story You've written in my life. Silence fear. Ignite boldness. Use my scars to set captives free. Let my life shout of Your mercy. In Jesus' name, Amen.

August 29
"Preach the Gospel at all times.
When necessary, use words."
St. Francis of Assisi

Son,
your life is a sermon louder than any microphone.
The way you love under pressure.
The way you stay pure in temptation.
The way you keep standing when others collapse.
These are your strongest sermons.

The world is not changed by clever arguments.
It is changed by warriors who bleed integrity,
who love without strings,
who walk through fire without losing their song.

Let your actions preach what your words can only echo.
Live a life so fierce in grace, so relentless in truth,
that even the deaf hear the sound of redemption roaring
through you.

"In the same way, let your light shine before others, that they may see your good deeds and glorify your Father in heaven." — Matthew 5:16

Daily Challenge: Choose one action today that will preach louder than any words you could speak.

Warrior's Prayer:
Father, let my life preach louder than my lips. Let my love be louder than my opinions. Shape my character into a living testimony of Your grace and power. Let every step shout Your goodness. In Jesus' name, Amen.

August 30
"The darker the night, the brighter the stars."
Fyodor Dostoevsky

Son,
darkness is not the absence of My light—it is the canvas for it.
The darker the battlefield around you becomes,
the brighter I will blaze through you.

The night cannot overcome you if your fire is fed.
Fear cannot silence you if your hope is rooted.
You were born to shine in warzones, not just in sanctuaries.

Do not curse the darkness.
Set it ablaze.
Stand tall.
Shine bright.
Let the broken world see what a Son of God looks like fully alive in enemy territory.

"The light shines in the darkness, and the darkness has not overcome it." — John 1:5

Daily Challenge: When you face a difficult moment today, see it as a chance to shine brighter, not shrink back.

Warrior's Prayer:
Father, set my spirit ablaze in the darkest places. Teach me to stand tall when the night falls heavy. Let my life burn so fiercely for You that no darkness can overcome it. In Jesus' name, Amen.

August 31

"A holy life will make the deepest impression. Lighthouses blow no horns; they only shine."
D.L. Moody

Son,
every step you take is writing a story.
Every choice you make is shaping a message.
What will it say?

Let your life preach hope when the world preaches despair.
Let your courage light up battlefields.
Let your perseverance inspire men to keep fighting when they want to quit.

You were not made to blend in.
You were made to be a living, breathing, walking declaration that God is real, love is fierce, and victory is unstoppable.

Write a story with your life that shakes the gates of hell.
Make every chapter echo through eternity.

"Whatever you do, work at it with all your heart, as working for the Lord, not for human masters." — Colossians 3:23

Daily Challenge: Live today as if your life is the clearest Gospel some people will ever read—because it is.

Warrior's Prayer:
Father, let my life be a message of Your relentless love, Your reckless mercy, and Your unstoppable power. Write Your story through every breath I take. I want my life to make Heaven roar and hell tremble. In Jesus' name, Amen.

September 1

"God is looking for those with whom He can do the impossible—what a pity that we plan only the things we can do by ourselves."
A.W. Tozer

Son,

you were not created for average plans, for safe dreams, for manageable missions. You were crafted for the impossible. You were designed to need Me. You were wired for battles where My strength is the only explanation for your victory.

When you only attempt what you can do, you shrink your destiny to the size of your own ability. But when you dare to step into the impossible with Me, you release Heaven's arsenal into earth's warfare. The impossible is My natural battleground.

Dream bigger. Pray louder. Move faster toward things that terrify your flesh but set your spirit on fire. I am the God of the impossible. And you are My son.

"For nothing will be impossible with God." — Luke 1:37

Daily Challenge: Identify one dream or goal you've thought was "too impossible"—and today, pray boldly over it as if God plans to move.

Warrior's Prayer:
Father, stretch my vision until it terrifies fear. Teach me to dream dreams so big they require Your hand to succeed. Let my life showcase Your impossible power in a broken world. In Jesus' name, Amen.

September 2

"Worry does not empty tomorrow of its sorrow. It empties today of its strength."
Corrie ten Boom

Son,
worry is a thief dressed in concern. It will promise you protection but steal your peace. It will promise you control but bind you in chains. It will exhaust you before the real battle even begins.

You cannot fight well today while carrying the weight of tomorrow. Trust Me with the future. Trust Me with the unknowns. Trust Me with the outcomes. Your call is not to predict every danger, but to stand ready, heart steady, eyes fixed on Me.

I give you daily bread for a reason. I will give you daily strength too. Fear robs the present. Faith fuels it.

"Therefore do not worry about tomorrow, for tomorrow will worry about itself. Each day has enough trouble of its own." — Matthew 6:34

Daily Challenge: Each time a worry rises today, immediately counter it by speaking a promise from God's Word aloud.

Warrior's Prayer:
Father, I release tomorrow into Your hands. I take hold of Your strength for today. Teach me to live fully present, fully trusting, and fully armed with faith. I refuse to waste today's strength on tomorrow's fears. In Jesus' name, Amen.

September 3

*"Success is not final, failure is not fatal: it is the
courage to continue that counts."*
Winston Churchill

Son,
your success today
does not guarantee victory tomorrow.
And your failure today
does not cancel destiny tomorrow.

The fight is daily.
The courage is hourly.
The call is constant:
Rise again.
Move again.
Believe again.

Your worth is not tied
to your last triumph
or your last stumble.
Your worth is anchored
in Me.

I am the God of new mercies,
new strength,
new fire—
every single morning.

Stay in the fight, son.
Stay in the fire.
Stay in the story.

"Because of the Lord's great love we are not consumed, for His compassions never fail. They are new every morning." — Lamentations 3:22–23

Daily Challenge: Reset today—let go of yesterday's victories and yesterday's failures. Begin again fiercely

Warrior's Prayer:
Father, teach me the courage to continue—whether the road is marked by success or struggle. Let me wake up each day ready to fight again, fueled by Your fresh mercy. I will not quit. I will not coast. In Jesus' name, Amen.

September 4

"The safest place to be is in the center of God's will."
Corrie ten Boom

Son,

safety is not the absence of danger. It is the absolute presence of destiny. You could be in the storm's eye, the battlefield's worst fire, the world's fiercest hatred—and still be safer in My will than hiding in a cave of fear.

My will doesn't always feel comfortable. But it is always unbreakable.

When you stand where I place you, no bullet, no betrayal, no scheme of hell can touch what I have sealed. My will may cost you everything. But it will give you everything that truly matters.

Plant your feet, son. Armor up. Walk the line I drew for you. Safety isn't the absence of struggle—it's standing in the center of My sovereign plan.

"The name of the Lord is a fortified tower; the righteous run to it and are safe." — Proverbs 18:10

Daily Challenge: Recommit today to standing wherever God has placed you—no matter how risky it feels.

Warrior's Prayer:
Father, anchor me in the center of Your will. Teach me that true safety isn't found in comfort but in obedience. I trust Your positioning more than I trust my perception. Let me fight faithfully wherever You plant me. In Jesus' name, Amen.

September 5

*"He is no fool who gives what he cannot keep
to gain what he cannot lose."*
Jim Elliot

Son,
every day the world tempts you to cling—to possessions, to status, to comfort, to control. But I am calling you to a deeper freedom: the freedom found in letting go.

You cannot keep anything this world promises. You cannot anchor your hope in shifting sands. But everything you surrender into My hands becomes a seed planted in eternity. Every act of faith becomes a flame in Heaven's halls.

Give boldly. Love recklessly. Forgive freely. Serve fiercely. Lose your life for My sake—and find it roaring back alive, unbreakable and unstoppable.

"For whoever wants to save their life will lose it, but whoever loses their life for Me will save it." — Luke 9:24

Daily Challenge: Practice letting go today—release one thing you're clinging to, and place it fully in God's hands.

Warrior's Prayer:
Father, pry my hands off anything not meant to carry into eternity. Teach me to hold earthly things loosely and heavenly things tightly. I want to lose my life in You—and find a life no enemy can steal. In Jesus' name, Amen.

September 6

"The Christian ideal has not been tried and found wanting. It has been found difficult; and left untried."
G.K. Chesterton

Son,
I did not call you to easy.
I called you to extraordinary.
Following Me will feel like swimming upstream in a world rushing toward destruction.
It will demand courage when comfort would be easier.
It will demand sacrifice when selfishness would feel safer.

Many have turned away—not because I failed them, but because they feared the cost.
But you, son—you were made to endure.
You were made to walk narrow roads and climb steep cliffs.
You were made to choose the harder right over the easier wrong.

When you find yourself facing a wall of resistance, don't turn back.
Press harder.
Stand firmer.
Live louder.
The path is hard—but it leads to a victory no enemy can steal.

"But small is the gate and narrow the road that leads to life, and only a few find it." — Matthew 7:14

Daily Challenge: Choose today to lean into a hard, right decision instead of an easy, wrong one.

Warrior's Prayer:
Father, I will not abandon the hard road. Strengthen my feet to climb when the way is steep. Build in me a heart that embraces sacrifice for the sake of Your glory. Let my life echo the strength of a faithful son. In Jesus' name, Amen.

September 7

*"A man is no fool who forsakes what he cannot keep
to gain what he cannot lose."*
Jim Elliot

Son,
what you cling to will either crown you or crush you.
The world will lure you to chase what glitters—fame,
fortune, fleeting pleasures.
But all of it turns to dust in the end.

I am offering you a trade—your temporary treasures for
eternal ones.
Your fading applause for everlasting honor.
Your short-lived security for unshakable glory.

You lose nothing when you give Me everything.
You gain everything that truly matters when you surrender it
all.
Don't live for what slips through your fingers.
Live for what builds a legacy hell can't touch.

"Store up for yourselves treasures in heaven, where moths and vermin do not destroy, and where thieves do not break in and steal." — Matthew 6:20

Daily Challenge: Give something today—time, resources, or energy—to invest in eternity instead of temporary success.

Warrior's Prayer:
Father, teach me to hold this world loosely and cling to You fiercely. I want to spend my life chasing treasures that will echo through eternity. Burn away every attachment that dims my fire for You. In Jesus' name, Amen.

September 8

"Hardships often prepare ordinary people for an extraordinary destiny."
C.S. Lewis

Son,
the fire you hate
is forging the strength you'll need.

The trials you fear
are sharpening the sword you will wield.

The pain you dread
is hollowing out the space for deeper joy.

Ordinary men
become extraordinary warriors
not through ease,
but through endurance.

Let the hardship have its work.
Let it carve you,
refine you,
build in you
a spirit that hell cannot break.

You are not being punished.
You are being prepared.

"Consider it pure joy, my brothers and sisters, whenever you face trials of many kinds, because you know that the testing of your faith produces perseverance." — James 1:2–3

Daily Challenge: Reframe a current hardship today—thank God for how He's using it to strengthen you.

Warrior's Prayer:
Father, teach me to see hardship not as punishment, but as preparation. Sharpen me through every fire. Forge a spirit in me that endures beyond every trial. Let perseverance mark my life. In Jesus' name, Amen.

September 9

"To be a Christian means to forgive the inexcusable because God has forgiven the inexcusable in you."
C.S. Lewis

Son,
forgiveness is not weakness—it is warfare.
It breaks chains not just around others—but around your own soul.

The enemy wants you to carry bitterness like a shield,
thinking it protects you.
But it only poisons you.
Forgiveness is laying down the weapon of revenge and picking up the sword of grace.
It does not mean you forget the pain—but you refuse to let it become your prison.

I forgave you freely, fully, fiercely.
And I am calling you to do the same.
Forgive radically.
Forgive repeatedly.
Forgive as one who has been rescued from the unpayable debt of sin.

"Bear with each other and forgive one another... Forgive as the Lord forgave you." — Colossians 3:13

Daily Challenge: Forgive someone today—even if they haven't apologized, even if they don't deserve it.

Warrior's Prayer:
Father, release my heart from the chains of bitterness. Teach me to forgive as fiercely and freely as You forgave me. Let my life be marked by radical grace that reflects Your mercy. In Jesus' name, Amen.

September 10
"We can certainly conquer it."
Caleb (Numbers 13:30)

Son,
courage does not mean the absence of fear.
It means choosing obedience even when fear roars loudest.

When you pray in the middle of trembling hands, when you move forward with knees shaking, when you declare My promises with a voice that quivers—you are standing in true courage.

I don't need perfect bravery.
I call for faithful steps.
I meet you in your weakness and flood you with My strength.

Let your prayers be your war cries.
Let your obedience be your shield.
Courage is not born in comfort—it is born in communion with Me.

"Be strong and courageous. Do not be afraid or terrified because of them, for the Lord your God goes with you."
— Deuteronomy 31:6

Daily Challenge: Step forward today in one area where fear has tried to paralyze you—pray first, then move.

Warrior's Prayer:
Father, teach me that courage is not the absence of fear but the triumph of faith. Let my prayers fuel my bravery. Lead me into bold action today, trusting Your presence with every step. In Jesus' name, Amen.

September 11

"If you are going through hell, keep going."
Winston Churchill

Son,
storms don't last forever.
But warriors don't wait them out—they walk through them.

Hell wants you to stop halfway.
Wants you to lay down your sword.
Wants you to believe the valley is your grave.
But valleys are only passageways for sons who keep moving.

You were not built to camp in defeat.
You were not made to set up shelter in sorrow.
You were forged to walk through fire and emerge stronger,
bolder, more dangerous to darkness than when you entered.

Don't stop in the middle, son.
Don't quit because it hurts.
Press your heel harder into the battlefield.
The other side is closer than you think.

"Even though I walk through the valley of the shadow of death, I will fear no evil, for You are with me."
— Psalm 23:4

Daily Challenge: Refuse to quit today—choose perseverance where you feel most tempted to give up.

Warrior's Prayer:
Father, when the valley closes in, teach me to walk through with my head high and my spirit unshaken. Strengthen my steps. Sharpen my faith. I will not camp in despair—I will walk through it by Your power. In Jesus' name, Amen.

September 12

*"You have never been unloved for a single
second of your life."*
Max Lucado

Son,
before you breathed your first breath, I loved you.
Before you fought your first battle, I chose you.
Before you stumbled your first step, I called you.

Your worth is not based on your victories or your failures.
It's not measured by the applause of men or the approval of the world.
It's anchored in the unbreakable, relentless, blood-sealed love I have placed upon you.

There is nothing you can do to make Me love you more.
There is nothing you can do to make Me love you less.
You fight not for My love—you fight from it.

Wear My love like armor, son.
It makes you bulletproof to shame.

"I have loved you with an everlasting love; I have drawn you with unfailing kindness." — Jeremiah 31:3

Daily Challenge: Today, when the voice of shame whispers, respond aloud: "I am fiercely loved by my Father."

Warrior's Prayer:
Father, drown every voice of shame with the roar of Your love. Anchor my heart in the unshakable truth that I am chosen, loved, and secured by You. I move forward today fully covered by Your love. In Jesus' name, Amen.

September 13

"Faith is the refusal to panic."
Martyn Lloyd-Jones

Son,
faith isn't just what you believe.
It's how you bleed when the sword strikes.
It's how you breathe when the storm breaks.
It's how you move
when fear howls in your ears.

Faith is the steady hand
that refuses to flinch.

The strong heart
that refuses to race.

The fierce spirit
that refuses to panic.

I did not call you to live frantic.
I called you to live anchored.
Anchored in promises deeper than storms.
Anchored in a Kingdom unshakable.

Panic is a liar.
Faith is your anthem.

Hold the line.

"You will keep in perfect peace those whose minds are steadfast, because they trust in You." — Isaiah 26:3

Daily Challenge: When you feel panic rising today, pause and declare: "My God reigns even here."

Warrior's Prayer:
Father, build an unflinching faith in me. Teach me to stand steady when fear screams loudest. Let panic find no foothold in my heart. You are my peace, my anchor, my fortress. In Jesus' name, Amen.

September 14
"Character is who you are when no one is watching."
John Wooden

Son,
your real strength isn't built in front of crowds.
It's built in the silence, the secrecy, the unseen.

The man you are behind closed doors—the man who prays
when no one applauds, who chooses integrity when
compromise looks easier—that is the man who wins real
battles.

Reputation is what others see.
Character is what Heaven sees.
Character is what demons fear.

Train your spirit in the dark places.
Let faithfulness be your reflex.
Let righteousness be your native language.
You are not performing for men—you are preparing for
eternity.

I see it all.
I reward it all.

"The eyes of the Lord are everywhere, keeping watch on the wicked and the good." — Proverbs 15:3

Daily Challenge: Choose to honor God today in one hidden way—something only He and you will know about.

Warrior's Prayer:
Father, shape my character in the secret places. Build a man inside me who needs no audience, no applause, and no approval except Yours. Let me be the same warrior in the dark that I am in the light. In Jesus' name, Amen.

September 15

"The world has yet to see what God can do with a man fully surrendered to Him."
Dwight L. Moody

Son,
partial surrender builds partial fire.
Partial obedience builds partial victories.

I did not call you to half-measures.
I called you to a fire that consumes everything.
A life laid fully down.
A heart handed fully over.

When you surrender everything,
you lose nothing worth keeping—
and you gain a power the world cannot manufacture and hell cannot match.

Lay it all down today—your rights, your reputation, your reservations.
A surrendered man is a dangerous man in the hands of God.

"Offer your bodies as a living sacrifice, holy and pleasing to God—this is your true and proper worship."
— Romans 12:1

Daily Challenge: Ask God today: "Is there any area I'm still holding back from You?" Then act on what He shows you.

Warrior's Prayer:
Father, I lay everything at Your feet—my dreams, my fears, my ambitions, my life. Ignite a fire in me that burns away everything less than Your will. Make me a man fully surrendered and fully alive in Your hands. In Jesus' name, Amen.

September 16
*"The will of God will not take us where the
grace of God cannot sustain us."*
Billy Graham

Son,
wherever I send you,
My grace has already prepared the ground beneath your feet.

You may walk through fire, but the flames will not consume you.
You may be thrust into battles bigger than your ability,
but My strength will be the shield around your spirit.

Fear will tell you you're abandoned.
Faith will tell you you're sustained.
I do not send My sons into wars alone.
I go before you, stand beside you, and guard your rear.

If I call you to it, I will carry you through it.
That's not just a promise.
It's a blood-sealed covenant.

"My grace is sufficient for you, for My power is made perfect in weakness." — 2 Corinthians 12:9

Daily Challenge: Step boldly into something today you've been hesitating over—trust God's sustaining grace.

Warrior's Prayer:
Father, if You have called me to it, I trust You to sustain me through it. Strengthen my hands for every battle, my heart for every test, and my spirit for every climb. Let me lean fully into Your grace today. In Jesus' name, Amen.

September 17

"The greatest danger is not that we aim too high and miss it, but that we aim too low and reach it."
Michelangelo

Son,
small dreams don't glorify a limitless God.
Safe prayers don't shake nations.
Tamed faith doesn't trouble the gates of hell.

You were not born to exist—you were born to advance.
You were not made to coast—you were made to conquer.

Aim higher, son.
Believe bigger.
Pray bolder.
Dream so dangerously that only Heaven's armies can accomplish it.

You are a son of the King.
Do not live like a beggar when I've crowned you for battle.

"Now to Him who is able to do immeasurably more than all we ask or imagine..." — Ephesians 3:20

Daily Challenge: Today, stretch one dream or prayer higher than you're comfortable with—and dare to believe God for it.

Warrior's Prayer:
Father, forgive me for aiming too small. Ignite my spirit to believe for battles worth fighting, mountains worth climbing, and victories worth shouting for Your glory. Let my life demand an explanation only You can satisfy. In Jesus' name, Amen.

September 18

"Relying on God has to begin all over again every day as if nothing had yet been done."
C.S. Lewis

Son,
faith is not a one-time decision.
It is a daily rebellion against fear.

You wake.
You choose.
You declare again:

"I will trust You today."

Not because yesterday's victories guarantee today's strength,
but because You are faithful today,
like You were yesterday,
and You will be tomorrow.

Faith isn't built once.
It's forged daily.

Breathe it in.
Speak it out.
Stand in it.

Begin again today, son.
Begin again in trust.

"His mercies are new every morning; great is Your faithfulness." — Lamentations 3:23

Daily Challenge: Before anything else today, stop and declare your trust aloud to God before stepping into your tasks.

Warrior's Prayer:
Father, I choose to trust You again today. Not leaning on yesterday's faith, but drawing fresh strength from Your unchanging mercy. Teach me to start each day as a new battlefield won by surrender. In Jesus' name, Amen.

September 19

*"You can never learn that Christ is all you need,
until Christ is all you have."*
Corrie ten Boom

Son,
you will never know the full weight of My sufficiency
until I strip away the idols you thought would sustain you.

I am not your backup plan.
I am not your safety net.
I am your source, your shield, your very breath.

When the applause fades, I remain.
When the riches dry up, I remain.
When the strength of your flesh fails, I remain.

When you reach the end of yourself,
you finally find the beginning of Me.

You were never meant to be enough on your own.
You were meant to live filled with a power the world cannot replicate.

"My flesh and my heart may fail, but God is the strength of my heart and my portion forever." — Psalm 73:26

Daily Challenge: Surrender one area today where you've been relying on your own strength instead of Christ's sufficiency.

Warrior's Prayer:
Father, strip away my idols and false securities. Bring me to the place where You are not just part of my strength—but my only strength. I trust You as my portion, my fortress, my everything. In Jesus' name, Amen.

September 20

*"The task ahead of you is never greater
than the power behind you."*
Ralph Waldo Emerson

Son,
you look at the mountain ahead and feel small.
You look at the battle lines drawn and feel outnumbered.

Good.
It forces you to remember: the battle is never won by human strength.
It is won by the Spirit of the Living God surging through willing vessels.

The task is heavy, yes.
The call is costly, yes.
But the power backing you is greater than any obstacle in front of you.

You don't fight alone.
You don't move alone.
You are backed by Heaven.

Step forward, son.
Not because you are strong enough—but because I AM.

"If God is for us, who can be against us?"
— Romans 8:31

Daily Challenge: Every time you feel overwhelmed today, say this out loud: "The power behind me is greater than the task ahead of me."

Warrior's Prayer:
Father, when I feel outmatched, remind me that I am backed by the armies of Heaven. Fill my spirit with the roar of Your strength. I move forward not in my power, but in Yours. In Jesus' name, Amen.

September 21

"You were made by God and for God, and until you understand that, life will never make sense."
Rick Warren

Son,
you were not created by accident.
You were handcrafted, heart-forged, mission-breathed into existence by Me.

You were not made for comfort.
You were made for conquest.
You were not made to chase approval.
You were made to carry My image into a broken world.

Until you root yourself in Me,
life will always feel restless.
Success will taste hollow.
Victory will feel empty.

Anchor yourself to your true origin:
My hands, My heart, My design.

Everything else flows from there.

"For in Him we live and move and have our being."
— Acts 17:28

Daily Challenge: Every time you feel aimless or anxious today, pause and declare: "I was made by God and for God."

Warrior's Prayer:
Father, root my identity in Your hands. Strip away every false label, every counterfeit identity. Let me live and move from the fierce truth that I am Yours, created for Your glory. In Jesus' name, Amen.

September 22
"We fear men so much, because we fear God so little."
William Gurnall

Son,
fear of man shrinks warriors into cowards.
Fear of man silences battle cries before they're ever sung.

You were not made to tremble before opinions.
You were not built to surrender your calling to applause or criticism.

Fear Me first, son—and all lesser fears will bow.
Revere My voice more than the voices of critics or crowds.
Stand taller because you kneel only before Me.

The fear of the Lord is not slavery—it is fierce freedom.
Freedom from compromise.
Freedom from comparison.
Freedom to live boldly, breathe deeply, and fight ruthlessly for what matters.

"The fear of the Lord is the beginning of wisdom."
— Proverbs 9:10

Daily Challenge: Every time you catch yourself fearing man today, immediately turn your focus back to fearing and honoring God alone.

Warrior's Prayer:
Father, teach me to fear You first and most. Strip away every fear of man. Make me deaf to the opinions of the crowd and fiercely alive to Your voice alone. Let me stand taller because I kneel only to You. In Jesus' name, Amen.

September 23
"If God is your partner, make your plans big."
D.L. Moody

Son,
small dreams
do not honor a limitless God.

If I am with you,
then dream mountains moved.
Dream nations reached.
Dream chains shattered.

Let your vision
outgrow your fears.
Let your faith
outpace your plans.
Risk bigger.
Pray louder.
Move faster.
You are not partnering with weakness.
You are partnering with the Almighty.

Plan big.
Pray bigger.
Move boldly.

I am with you, son.

> **"Commit to the Lord whatever you do, and He will establish your plans."** — Proverbs 16:3

Daily Challenge: Dream and pray over something today that feels too big for you—something that would demand God's power to happen.

Warrior's Prayer:
Father, expand my vision to match Your greatness. Break every ceiling of fear, hesitation, and small thinking. Teach me to plan with Heaven in mind and to move with boldness in Your strength. In Jesus' name, Amen.

September 24

"The world offers promises full of emptiness. God offers emptiness full of promise."
John Blanchard

Son,
the promises of the world are candy-coated lies—sweet for a moment, bitter for a lifetime.

Fame will not heal you.
Riches will not satisfy you.
Pleasure will not complete you.

But My promises?
They endure storms.
They outlast betrayals.
They fuel movements and awaken dead hearts.

I may call you into emptiness—into deserts, into waiting places, into sacrifice.
But I fill emptiness with life unstoppable.
The emptier your hands, the more room for My miracles.

Let the world keep its hollow crowns.
You were made for eternal treasure.

"He who promised is faithful." — Hebrews 10:23

Daily Challenge: Every time the world tempts you today with false promises, declare: "I choose the promises of God."

Warrior's Prayer:
Father, open my eyes to the emptiness behind the world's promises. Fill me instead with the richness of Your truth. Let my heart hunger for nothing less than the treasures You give. In Jesus' name, Amen.

September 25

"You will keep him in perfect peace, whose mind is stayed on You, because he trusts in You." — Isaiah 26:3

Son,
perfect peace is not found in perfect circumstances.
It's found in a fierce focus on Me.

You will be tempted to let your mind scatter—
to let it be filled with headlines, deadlines, regrets, and fears.

But peace comes when you fix your mind like a warrior's gaze—
steady, locked in, unshaken by the chaos.

Stay your mind on Me.
Glue your gaze to My Word.
Tether your heart to My promises.

The storm around you doesn't determine your peace.
The anchor within you does.

"You will keep him in perfect peace, whose mind is stayed on You, because he trusts in You." — Isaiah 26:3

Daily Challenge: Throughout the day today, when your mind starts to scatter, stop and declare: "My mind is stayed on the Lord."

Warrior's Prayer:
Father, anchor my mind to You today. When fear, distraction, and chaos try to pull me apart, pull me deeper into Your peace. Let my thoughts be a fortress of trust in You alone. In Jesus' name, Amen.

September 26
"Do not pray for easy lives. Pray to be stronger men."
Phillips Brooks

Son,
I never promised easy.
I promised empowerment.
I promised endurance.
I promised My Spirit breathing through your weakness,
roaring through your battles.

The world prays for lighter loads.
You are called to pray for a stronger back.
The world begs for calmer seas.
You are called to ask for a fiercer spirit.

I'm not raising you to run from the fire.
I'm raising you to walk through it—untouched, unbowed,
unbreakable.

Easy paths build soft men.
Hard paths build heroes.

"Endure hardship as discipline; God is treating you as His children." — Hebrews 12:7

Daily Challenge: Stop today and pray, "Father, don't remove the challenge—make me stronger through it."

Warrior's Prayer:
Father, I will not beg for an easier life. I ask instead for a stronger heart. Forge a warrior spirit in me through every trial. Let hardship build endurance, courage, and an unshakable trust in You. In Jesus' name, Amen.

September 27
"Attempt something so great for God that it's doomed to fail unless God is in it."
John Haggai

Son,
the size of your dreams reflects the size of your faith.
And small dreams are an insult to a limitless God.

I did not save you for safe living.
I redeemed you for reckless obedience.
For holy risk.
For mountains that mock logic.
For seas that split at My command.

Attempt the ridiculous, the impossible, the unthinkable for My glory.
If it's too small for faith, it's too small for you.

Dream bigger.
Move bolder.
Attempt what will only succeed if I show up.

"With God all things are possible." — Matthew 19:26

Daily Challenge: Write down one crazy-big faith goal today—and begin praying and planning toward it.

Warrior's Prayer:
Father, shatter every boundary I've placed on Your power. Teach me to live and dream in ways that require Your hand, not just my effort. I want to attempt things so bold that only You can bring them to life. In Jesus' name, Amen.

September 28
"Courage, dear heart."
C.S. Lewis

Son,
when the darkness thickens,
when the battle drags long,
when the voices of defeat grow loud—

courage, dear heart.

When you see no open doors,
no clear skies,
no easy paths—

courage, dear heart.

You are not abandoned.
You are not defeated.
You are not overlooked.

My hand is still steady.
My plan is still unfolding.
My presence is still surrounding you.

Take courage.
Not from circumstances—
but from My promises.

Courage, dear heart.
You are closer to victory than you know.

"Be strong and take heart, all you who hope in the Lord."
— Psalm 31:24

Daily Challenge: Whenever you feel discouraged today, whisper aloud: "Courage, dear heart. My hope is in the Lord."

Warrior's Prayer:
Father, breathe courage into my spirit today. When fear presses heavy, flood my heart with hope. Teach me to anchor my courage not in what I see but in who You are. I trust You in the middle of the unknown. In Jesus' name, Amen.

September 29

"There are no shortcuts to any place worth going."
Beverly Sills

Son,
shortcut faith produces shallow warriors.
Fast-track victories create fragile legacies.

I am not interested in microwave success.
I am forging you in the slow fires of obedience, discipline, sacrifice.

Endurance matters more than speed.
Depth matters more than display.
Character matters more than applause.

Let the others race for quick wins.
You are called to build something eternal.
Slow.
Solid.
Unshakable.

The long road is hard—but it's holy.

"Let us not grow weary in doing good, for at the proper time we will reap a harvest if we do not give up."
— Galatians 6:9

Daily Challenge: Commit today to one discipline (prayer, Scripture, serving) that you'll keep building slowly, no matter how long it takes to see fruit.

Warrior's Prayer:
Father, burn out the impatience in me. Teach me the sacred strength of steady obedience. Build a legacy in my life that outlasts storms and outlives seasons. I choose the long road if it leads to You. In Jesus' name, Amen.

September 30
"The darker the night, the brighter the stars."
Fyodor Dostoevsky

Son,
darkness is not the end of the story—it's the stage for the brightest lights.

When the world seems lost,
you will shine stronger.
When hope seems crushed,
you will burn fiercer.
When faith seems foolish,
you will live louder.

Do not curse the darkness.
Be the fire that cannot be put out.

I made you to shine when others break.
I made you to rise when others fall.
I made you to carry the torch of My Kingdom into enemy territory—and win.

"You are the light of the world. A city set on a hill cannot be hidden." — Matthew 5:14

Daily Challenge: Shine brightly today through one bold act of kindness, truth, or encouragement—even if no one notices but God.

Warrior's Prayer:
Father, set my life ablaze with Your light. When darkness closes in, let me shine brighter, love harder, stand taller. Use me as a beacon that draws others to Your heart. In Jesus' name, Amen.

October 1
"Radical obedience is the gateway to radical impact."
Christine Caine

Son,
you will not make an eternal impact by living a life of casual obedience.
Half-hearted faith changes nothing.
Safe faith shakes nothing.

I am calling you to a deeper surrender—
the kind of obedience that doesn't wait for clarity, comfort, or consensus.

The world doesn't need more cautious believers.
It needs bold warriors willing to move when I whisper,
willing to risk everything when I command,
willing to stand even when it costs.

Radical obedience looks foolish to the world.
But it's fire in My hands.

"If you love Me, keep My commands." — John 14:15

Daily Challenge: Today, obey God immediately in one area where you've been hesitating.

Warrior's Prayer:
Father, ignite radical obedience in my spirit. Teach me to move when You speak, no matter how costly it looks. I don't want safe faith—I want surrendered faith. Use my yes to unleash Your power through my life. In Jesus' name, Amen.

October 2

"When God is all you have, you realize He's all you need."
Timothy Keller

Son,
sometimes I strip away the excess.
Sometimes I allow the crutches to break, the idols to fall, the walls to collapse—
not to punish you, but to purify you.

When all you have left is Me,
you finally see that I am enough.
Not barely enough—overflowingly, overwhelmingly enough.

I am not your last resort.
I am your first love, your sustaining strength, your endless supply.

Lean fully into Me, son.
You'll find I was never holding out on you.
I was holding you up the whole time.

> **"The Lord is my shepherd; I lack nothing."**
> — Psalm 23:1

Daily Challenge: If something feels stripped away today—comfort, security, control—thank God for using it to show you His sufficiency.

Warrior's Prayer:
Father, You are enough. Strip away every illusion that I need anything more than You. Teach me to drink deeply of Your strength when everything else fades. Anchor my soul in You alone. In Jesus' name, Amen.

October 3
"The way to be nothing is to do nothing."
Nathaniel Emmons

Son,
you were not made
to drift through life.

You were not crafted
to live tame,
play safe,
or die with your song unsung.

Do not confuse waiting
with wasting.
Do not confuse hesitation
with holiness.

Move.
Pray.
Build.
Battle.

I have placed a fire inside you
that was never meant
to stay silent.

Live fully.
Move boldly.
Fight fiercely.

Do something that makes hell tremble.

> **"Whatever you do, work at it with all your heart, as working for the Lord."** — *Colossians 3:23*

Daily Challenge: Take one bold action today toward a dream, calling, or mission God has placed in your heart.

Warrior's Prayer:
Father, kill the hesitation in me. Stir up the fire You planted inside my spirit. Teach me to live with urgency, to fight with passion, and to build with boldness for Your glory. In Jesus' name, Amen.

October 4

*"Success is not about what you accomplish,
but about who you become."*
Dallas Willard

*Son,
the world measures success by achievements, trophies, and titles.
But I measure it differently.*

*I'm not just building what you do.
I'm shaping who you become.*

*Victory isn't crossing a finish line faster than others.
Victory is crossing it with a heart that looks like Mine.*

*You could stack up worldly success and still be spiritually bankrupt.
Or you could walk a quieter road—and be celebrated in the halls of Heaven.*

*Chase character over accomplishment.
Chase holiness over hustle.
Chase My heart over earthly crowns.*

"Man looks at the outward appearance, but the Lord looks at the heart." — 1 Samuel 16:7

Daily Challenge: Spend 10 minutes today reflecting not on what you're achieving—but on who you're becoming.

Warrior's Prayer:
Father, shape me into a man after Your own heart. Teach me to value character above accolades. Refine my spirit until my life reflects Your goodness in every battle, every moment. In Jesus' name, Amen.

October 5

*"Joy is not the absence of suffering;
it is the presence of God."*
Elisabeth Elliot

Son,
joy isn't fragile.
It isn't circumstantial.
It's not chained to the rise and fall of your emotions.

True joy is a weapon.
It's rooted deep in My presence—
unshaken by storm, untouched by suffering, undimmed by delay.

Joy is a declaration to hell itself:
"I am not ruled by what I see—I am ruled by the One who reigns."

Carry My joy into every battle.
It will be your strength when the fight gets long.
It will be your shout when the shadows fall.

"The joy of the Lord is your strength." — Nehemiah 8:10

Daily Challenge: Choose to worship today not because everything is perfect, but because God is present.

Warrior's Prayer:
Father, plant unshakable joy in my spirit. Let it fuel me through every hardship, let it roar louder than fear, and let it strengthen my hands for the battles ahead. I fight today with joy burning in my bones. In Jesus' name, Amen.

October 6

"The measure of a life is not its duration but its donation."
Corrie ten Boom

Son,
life isn't measured in years lived—
it's measured in love given.
It's measured in burdens carried for others,
in silent sacrifices no one sees,
in souls lifted closer to My heart because you chose to show up.

The world chases long life.
I call you to chase deep life.
To bleed for causes that matter.
To serve where it's thankless.
To love where it costs.

Eternity will not weigh the length of your days—
it will weigh the weight of your obedience.

Live light to the world.
Live heavy for Heaven.

"Whoever wants to become great among you must be your servant." — Matthew 20:26

Daily Challenge: Look for one opportunity today to serve someone secretly, with no credit and no applause.

Warrior's Prayer:
Father, teach me to measure my life not by time, but by sacrifice. Make me a servant-warrior whose greatest victories are counted in lives touched, not trophies won. I want to live heavy for Your Kingdom. In Jesus' name, Amen.

October 7
*"You can never be too small for God to use—
only too full of yourself."*
Vance Havner

Son,
I do not require impressive résumés.
I am not searching for polished performers.
I am searching for surrendered hearts.

Pride is a wall I will not climb.
But humility is a gate wide open for My glory to flood through.

You will never be too broken, too battered, too inexperienced for Me to use you.
But you can be too proud.

Empty yourself, son.
Lay it all down—your titles, your fears, your need to be seen.
Stay small enough for Me to fill you.

Small men in the world's eyes become giants in My hands.

"God opposes the proud but shows favor to the humble."
— James 4:6

Daily Challenge: Choose humility today—apologize first, serve quietly, honor someone else above yourself.

Warrior's Prayer:
Father, strip away every layer of pride that blocks Your power from flowing through me. Teach me to stay small in the world's eyes but mighty in Your Spirit. I want to be an empty vessel You can fill without limit. In Jesus' name, Amen.

October 8

"Never be afraid to trust an unknown future to a known God."
Corrie ten Boom

Son,
you fear the pages not yet written.
You fear the battles not yet fought.

But I am already there.
Already at the next crossroads.
Already in the next battle.
Already at the mountaintop waiting for you.

The future is not a void.
It is filled with My presence.
It is drenched in My promises.
It is sealed with My sovereignty.

Walk forward, son.
Not blindly—
but boldly.
Not fearfully—
but faithfully.

The unknown to you
is already known to Me.

"For I know the plans I have for you,"
— Jeremiah 29:11a

Daily Challenge: Every time fear about the future rises today, declare: "My God is already there."

Warrior's Prayer:
Father, teach me to walk boldly into the unknown because I am never unknown to You. Anchor my heart in the confidence that You have already prepared the way. I choose trust over fear today. In Jesus' name, Amen.

October 9
"When we work, we work. When we pray, God works."
Hudson Taylor

Son,
your best human effort can move small mountains.
But prayer moves oceans.

You were not built to carry the mission alone.
You were built to unleash My hand into the battles you
cannot win by strategy or strength.

Prayer is not a last resort.
It is the first weapon.
The primary battle plan.
The secret artillery hell cannot defend against.

Stop fighting with empty hands.
Raise your hands.
Fill the sky with your cries.
Let Me move where your strength stops.

"Call to Me and I will answer you and tell you great and unsearchable things you do not know."
— Jeremiah 33:3

Daily Challenge: Spend focused, passionate time today asking God to move in one area you've been striving to control.

Warrior's Prayer:
Father, remind me that prayer is not passive—it is power. Teach me to unleash Your strength into the battles I cannot win by effort alone. I call on You today to move mountains I cannot climb. In Jesus' name, Amen.

October 10
"You are not fighting for victory—
you are fighting from victory."
Tony Evans

Son,
you are not charging into battle hoping to win.
You are moving forward because the war was already won at the Cross.

Every lie of the enemy is already defeated.
Every stronghold of darkness is already broken.
Every weapon formed against you has already been disarmed.

You do not fight alone.
You do not fight to maybe survive.
You fight to enforce a victory that is already signed in blood and sealed by resurrection.

Fight from victory, son.
Fight like the outcome is already guaranteed—because it is.

"But thanks be to God! He gives us the victory through our Lord Jesus Christ." — 1 Corinthians 15:57

Daily Challenge: Face today's battles with this mindset: "I'm not fighting for victory—I'm enforcing the victory already won."

Warrior's Prayer:
Father, burn into my heart the truth that I fight from victory, not for it. Let every prayer, every move, every battle roar with the confidence that You have already overcome. I enforce Your victory today. In Jesus' name, Amen.

October 11
"The only thing that can conquer fear is faith."
Woodrow Kroll

Son,
fear isn't fought with logic.
It isn't defeated by pretending it doesn't exist.
Fear bows to one thing: faith.

Faith that I am bigger than what you face.
Faith that I am working even when you can't see it.
Faith that the darkness doesn't get the final word.

You don't have to pretend you're fearless.
You just have to believe that I am greater.

Fear may roar—but faith roars louder.

"When I am afraid, I put my trust in You."
— Psalm 56:3

Daily Challenge: When fear rises today, say aloud: "Fear, you bow to my faith in the living God."

Warrior's Prayer:
Father, when fear rises, teach me to raise my shield of faith higher. Fill me with courage that comes not from my strength but from Your unstoppable power. Let faith roar louder than fear in my life today. In Jesus' name, Amen.

October 12

*"Your greatest ministry will flow out
of your deepest wounds."*
Rick Warren

Son,
I do not waste wounds.
I do not overlook tears.
I do not despise the scars you carry.

What broke you will become what fuels you.
What hurt you will become what heals others.

The world wants you to hide your pain.
I want you to hand it to Me—
so I can transform it into a sword.

Your ministry is not in your perfection.
It's in your redemption.

Let Me redeem it all, son.
Nothing is wasted in My hands.

"He heals the brokenhearted and binds up their wounds." — Psalm 147:3

Daily Challenge: Ask God today how He wants to use one of your past wounds to bring healing to someone else.

Warrior's Prayer:
Father, I give You every scar. Every story. Every broken place. Heal me so You can send me. Use my wounds not as weapons of shame, but as swords of freedom for others. In Jesus' name, Amen.

October 13

"The greatest battles are won on your knees."
Charles Spurgeon

Son,
you want to fight with fists.
You want to conquer with strength.

But real battles
are won in surrender.

Knees to the ground.
Hands lifted high.
Heart broken open before Me.

Victory is born
not from louder shouting—
but from deeper kneeling.

Hell trembles
when a warrior bows.
Heaven thunders
when a son cries out.

Kneel low today, son.
Rise in unstoppable power.

"The Lord is near to all who call on Him, to all who call on Him in truth." — Psalm 145:18

Daily Challenge: Physically kneel today and spend time in surrendered, desperate prayer.

Warrior's Prayer:
Father, teach me the power of kneeling low. Remind me that the fiercest battles are won in surrender, not striving. I choose to fight on my knees today, trusting You to bring the victory. In Jesus' name, Amen.

October 14
"You are free not by your striving but by His sacrifice."
John Piper

Son,
freedom doesn't come from trying harder.
It doesn't come from performing better.
It comes from trusting deeper.

You were not freed because you got it right.
You were freed because I paid the price.

You don't have to earn My love.
You don't have to work your way into My arms.
You fight from freedom, not for it.

Stop living chained to the lie that you have to prove yourself.
You are already loved.
Already chosen.
Already redeemed.

Now live like a man who is free.

"It is for freedom that Christ has set us free. Stand firm, then, and do not let yourselves be burdened again by a yoke of slavery." — Galatians 5:1

Daily Challenge: When guilt or shame whispers today, declare: "I am free because Christ set me free!"

Warrior's Prayer:
Father, teach me to live like a son who is already free. Break every chain of striving and shame. Let me walk boldly in the freedom You purchased with Your blood. I fight today not for approval but from Your victory. In Jesus' name, Amen.

October 15
"The future is as bright as the promises of God."
William Carey

Son,
the headlines will scream despair.
The crowds will shout fear.
But My promises still stand—bright, unbreakable,
unstoppable.

The world sees chaos.
You see covenant.

The world sees uncertainty.
You see destiny.

Anchor yourself not in the shifting tides of opinion, but in the solid rock of My Word.
I have promised.
I have spoken.
I will not fail.

Your future is not built on circumstances—
it's built on My character.

"For no matter how many promises God has made, they are 'Yes' in Christ." — 2 Corinthians 1:20

Daily Challenge: Pick one promise from Scripture today and declare it boldly over your life and future.

Warrior's Prayer:
Father, anchor my hope in Your promises, not the world's fears. Teach me to live forward, not with anxiety, but with unshakable faith that You are faithful. My future is bright because it is built on You. In Jesus' name, Amen.

October 16
"There is no pit so deep that God's love is not deeper still."
Corrie ten Boom

Son,
you may feel buried, forgotten, surrounded.
But I am deeper still.

You may walk through nights so black you can't see your own hands.
I am deeper still.

You may sit in ashes you never thought you'd taste.
I am deeper still.

There is no wound I cannot heal.
No shame I cannot wash.
No darkness My light cannot invade.

When you hit the bottom, you'll find My arms already underneath you.
I will not let you fall beyond My reach.

"Where can I go from Your Spirit? Where can I flee from Your presence?" — Psalm 139:7

Daily Challenge: Today, speak this aloud when discouragement rises: "God's love is deeper than this."

Warrior's Prayer:
Father, when the pit feels endless, remind me that Your love has no bottom. Rescue me. Hold me. Remind me that even when I cannot see You, You are already there. Deeper still. In Jesus' name, Amen.

October 17
"You can't be a warrior if you're unwilling to bleed."
Anonymous

Son,
real warriors don't fight because it's easy.
They fight because the cause is worth it.

You will bleed.
You will ache.
You will lose battles along the way.
But those wounds, carried well, will become your testimony.

If you're afraid of the scars, you'll never wield the sword.

The greatest warriors are the ones who learned that scars are not signs of defeat—
they're proof you stayed in the fight.

Bleed if you must.
But never bow to defeat.

"Fight the good fight of the faith. Take hold of the eternal life to which you were called."
— 1 Timothy 6:12

Daily Challenge: Endure discomfort today for a higher purpose—don't back down when it costs you something.

Warrior's Prayer:
Father, forge in me a spirit willing to bleed for what matters. Teach me to wear my scars not with shame, but with honor. I am not afraid of the cost if You are my prize. Strengthen me to fight well and finish strong. In Jesus' name, Amen.

October 18

"What lies behind us and what lies before us are tiny matters compared to what lies within us."
Ralph Waldo Emerson

Son,
your past does not define you.
Your future does not intimidate Me.

It is what lies within you
that matters most.

The Spirit of the Living God—
the fire of unquenchable purpose—
the roar of resurrection life.

It is not your history
or your enemies
that determine your destiny.

It is the flame inside you.

Tend it.
Feed it.
Unleash it.

You carry more than memories.
You carry My very breath.

"He who is in you is greater than he who is in the world."
— 1 John 4:4

Daily Challenge: Speak life into yourself today. Declare over yourself: "God's Spirit in me is greater than anything against me."

Warrior's Prayer:
Father, strengthen the fire inside me. Remind me that my history and my fears do not dictate my future. Your Spirit defines me. Your power fills me. Let the world see Your greatness burning through my life. In Jesus' name, Amen.

October 19

*"Faith is not the absence of doubt, but rather
the means to overcome it."*
Paul Tillich

Son,
I am not asking you to see the entire journey.
I am asking you to trust Me with the next step.

You don't have to map out the mountain.
You don't have to predict every storm.
You just have to lift your foot in obedience.

Faith is not fueled by full clarity—it's fueled by full trust.

I don't promise to show you the whole staircase.
I promise to steady you with every step you take in My name.

Move, even when the way looks impossible.
I am already carving the path beneath your feet.

"For we walk by faith, not by sight." — 2 Corinthians 5:7

Daily Challenge: Take one act of obedience today even if you can't see the full result yet—trust God to meet you there.

Warrior's Prayer:
Father, I trust You even when the road ahead is hidden. Strengthen my spirit to step boldly, not because I see everything, but because I know You are leading. I walk by faith today, one step at a time. In Jesus' name, Amen.

October 20
"God is most glorified in us when we are most satisfied in Him."
John Piper

Son,
true satisfaction isn't found in success, approval, or achievement.
It's found in Me.

The world will pull at your appetite—offering shallow pleasures, temporary crowns.
But none of it will ever fill the fire in your spirit.

Only My presence satisfies.
Only My love fulfills.
Only My calling ignites the life you were born to live.

When you are satisfied in Me, your life roars louder than any sermon.
When you are anchored in Me, the storms can rage but your heart will sing.

I am your portion.
I am your prize.
I am enough.

"Whom have I in heaven but You? And earth has nothing I desire besides You." — Psalm 73:25

Daily Challenge: Pause today to worship God not for what He gives, but simply for who He is.

Warrior's Prayer:
Father, make You the deepest desire of my heart. Satisfy me more than success, more than applause, more than comfort. Let my life glorify You by finding all my joy in Your presence. In Jesus' name, Amen.

October 21

*"The greater your knowledge of the goodness and grace of
God on your life, the more likely you are to
praise Him in the storm."*
Matt Chandler

Son,
storms are inevitable.
The battle will rage.
But praise is your weapon.

Praise doesn't wait for the clouds to clear.
Praise doesn't depend on perfect outcomes.
Praise declares My goodness even in the fiercest fire.

When you praise Me in the middle of the chaos,
you strip the enemy of one of his greatest weapons: fear.

Worship isn't weakness—it's warfare.
It is the defiant roar of a son who knows his Father cannot fail.

"I will bless the Lord at all times; His praise shall continually be in my mouth." — Psalm 34:1

Daily Challenge: No matter what hits you today, stop and praise God for who He is—out loud.

Warrior's Prayer:
Father, let praise be my battle cry. Teach me to bless Your name not just after the storm, but inside it. Fill my mouth with declarations of Your goodness no matter what the battlefield looks like. In Jesus' name, Amen.

October 22
"If you can see it, it's temporary. If you can't, it's eternal."
A.W. Tozer

Son,
everything you see around you—
the crowds, the trophies, the headlines—
it's all fading.

The unseen is what matters most.
The battles you fight in prayer.
The faith you anchor when no one watches.
The character you build in the hidden places.

Live for what lasts.
Sow into what will echo into eternity.
Fight for the crowns that cannot rot or rust.

Your real victories are measured in unseen realms.

"So we fix our eyes not on what is seen, but on what is unseen, since what is seen is temporary, but what is unseen is eternal." — 2 Corinthians 4:18

Daily Challenge: Make one choice today that invests in eternity, not just in temporary comfort or success.

Warrior's Prayer:
Father, fix my eyes on the eternal. Strip away every attachment to what fades. Teach me to live with Heaven in view and eternity in my heart. Let me fight for what matters most. In Jesus' name, Amen.

October 23

*"God's work done in God's way will
never lack God's supply."*
Hudson Taylor

Son,
you worry about provision.
You fear running dry.
You fear the gaps, the lack, the needs.

But where I guide,
I provide.

Where I call,
I equip.

Where I lead,
I pour rivers into deserts.

You do not have to manufacture miracles.
You only have to obey.

Provision follows purpose.

Faith draws water from the rock.
Obedience unleashes Heaven's storehouses.

Do not chase supply.
Chase Me.
And everything you need will find you.

"And my God will meet all your needs according to the riches of His glory in Christ Jesus." — Philippians 4:19

Daily Challenge: Trust God today for one area where you've been tempted to strive instead of surrender.

Warrior's Prayer:
Father, I trust Your provision for every step You call me to take. Silence my striving. Calm my anxious hands. Let my faith draw from Your endless supply. I will move boldly, trusting You to meet me there. In Jesus' name, Amen.

October 24

"Trust the past to God's mercy, the present to God's love, and the future to God's providence."
St. Augustine

Son,
no man and no enemy can shorten your mission.
Your days are numbered by My hand, not theirs.

You are not at the mercy of chance.
You are not a victim of fate.
You are a son carrying out a divine assignment.

When you walk with Me,
you are untouchable until your race is finished.

Fear does not determine your finish line.
My purpose does.

Live boldly, son.
Speak louder.
Move faster.
Fight harder.
Death only comes when destiny is complete.

"All the days ordained for me were written in Your book before one of them came to be." — Psalm 139:16

Daily Challenge: Live boldly today—act, speak, love without fear of what might happen.

Warrior's Prayer:
Father, teach me to live as one sent and secured by Your hand. Anchor my courage in the truth that my life is held by You alone. Until my assignment is complete, I will live with fearless boldness. In Jesus' name, Amen.

October 25

"Being a Christian is less about cautiously avoiding sin than about courageously and actively doing God's will."
Dietrich Bonhoeffer

Son,
you were not made to waste your strength chasing shadows.
You were not crafted to climb ladders that lead to nowhere.

The enemy doesn't just tempt you to fail—
he tempts you to succeed at the wrong things.

You could win applause and miss your assignment.
You could gather treasures and forfeit your soul.

Stay laser-focused on the mission I gave you:
Build what matters.
Fight for what lasts.
Live for the applause of Heaven.

Success in the wrong kingdom is still failure.

"What good will it be for someone to gain the whole world, yet forfeit their soul?" — Matthew 16:26

Daily Challenge: Evaluate your goals today—adjust one if it's more about earthly success than eternal impact.

Warrior's Prayer:
Father, sharpen my vision. Align my dreams with Your destiny for me. Protect me from wasting my strength on things that don't matter. Teach me to succeed in the only Kingdom that endures forever. In Jesus' name, Amen.

October 26

"To be a Christian without prayer is no more possible than to be alive without breathing."
Martin Luther

Son,
prayer is not a nice addition to your life.
It is your life.

You breathe by prayer.
You fight by prayer.
You rise by prayer.
You endure by prayer.

Cut off prayer—and your spirit suffocates.
Ignite prayer—and your spirit roars.

Prayer is not preparation for the battle.
Prayer is the battle.

Breathe deep today, son.
Fill your lungs with the power of communion with Me.
Without it, you survive.
With it, you conquer.

"Pray without ceasing." — 1 Thessalonians 5:17

Daily Challenge: Set intentional alarms today to pause and breathe prayer over your life, your family, and your mission.

Warrior's Prayer:
Father, make prayer my first weapon, my constant breath, my daily power. Let my heart beat in rhythm with Yours. Teach me to live with prayer as my lifeline and my battle cry. In Jesus' name, Amen.

October 27

"The man who mobilizes the Christian church to pray will make the greatest contribution to world evangelization in history."
Andrew Murray

Son,
your private prayers are part of a global war.
Every whispered intercession shakes unseen kingdoms.
Every unseen battle cry on your knees ripples across nations.

You don't pray alone.
You stand shoulder-to-shoulder with an army of warriors across the earth.
You light fires in places you may never see.
You shift destinies through faith-filled words.

Mobilize yourself first.
Mobilize others next.

Awaken the sleeping soldiers.
Prayer is not the last resort—it is the launching ground of revolutions.

"The prayer of a righteous person is powerful and effective." — James 5:16

Daily Challenge: Pray specifically today for a person, a country, or a cause that desperately needs revival—and believe it matters.

Warrior's Prayer:
Father, ignite my prayers with power. Let me stand in the gap for the broken, the lost, and the bound. Make my private battles in prayer a public victory for Your Kingdom. Wake up the warriors through my faithfulness. In Jesus' name, Amen.

October 28
*"Expect great things from God; attempt
great things for God."*
William Carey

*Son,
you limit yourself
when you limit Me.*

*Expect more.
Pray louder.
Move faster.*

*Stop playing small
when I am the God of seas split,
mountains moved,
tombs emptied.*

*I did not save you for safety.
I saved you for exploits.
I saved you for battles that make angels lean in.*

*Attempt the great.
Attempt the impossible.
Attempt the ridiculous.*

I will meet you there.

"Now to Him who is able to do immeasurably more than all we ask or imagine..." — Ephesians 3:20

Daily Challenge: Attempt one bold act today—something that if God doesn't show up, it won't succeed.

Warrior's Prayer:
Father, stretch my prayers and stretch my steps. Teach me to expect greater things from Your hand and to attempt greater things by Your Spirit. I refuse to live small when You have called me to live bold. In Jesus' name, Amen.

October 29

"The highest form of worship is the worship of unselfish Christian service."
Billy Graham

Son,
songs matter.
Prayers matter.
But worship is bigger than your words—it's your life.

When you serve with no strings attached, you are singing louder than a thousand choirs.
When you lift another man's burden, you lift a song to Heaven.

Real worship is when your hands are dirty with service,
your heart is bleeding with compassion,
your life is surrendered in action.

Serve like it's sacred—because it is.

"Whatever you did for one of the least of these brothers and sisters of Mine, you did for Me." — Matthew 25:40

Daily Challenge: Find a small, real way to serve someone today—not for applause, but for God's glory.

Warrior's Prayer:
Father, let my life be a living song of worship. Teach me that true service to others is sacred ground. Fill my hands with compassion and my heart with humility as I serve today. In Jesus' name, Amen.

October 30
"Obedience is the key that opens every door."
C.S. Lewis

Son,
blessing doesn't follow talent.
It doesn't follow appearance, wealth, or connections.

Blessing follows obedience.

You want open doors?
Obey.
You want favor?
Obey.
You want supernatural strength in impossible places?
Obey.

I am not impressed by giftedness.
I am moved by surrendered yeses.

Obedience opens gates no man can close.

"Blessed rather are those who hear the word of God and obey it." — Luke 11:28

Daily Challenge: Obey immediately today in one area where you know God is prompting you—no delay.

Warrior's Prayer:
Father, train my spirit to obey instantly, not reluctantly. Show me the doors that obedience will unlock in my life. Let my life roar YES to Your voice today without hesitation. In Jesus' name, Amen.

October 31
"When Satan reminds you of your past,
remind him of his future."
Adrian Rogers

Son,
the enemy loves to replay your mistakes.
He loves to throw your failures in your face.
He loves to whisper that you are your worst moment.

But he is a liar.
And his time is running out.

When guilt rises, raise the banner of grace higher.
When shame attacks, lift your eyes to the empty tomb.

You are not defined by your past—you are defined by the victory of Christ.

And the enemy?
His doom is already sealed.

You fight from a victory he can never reverse.

"There is now no condemnation for those who are in Christ Jesus." — Romans 8:1

Daily Challenge: Every time a regret or old failure surfaces today, declare: "I am redeemed. Satan is defeated."

Warrior's Prayer:
Father, silence every voice of shame with the shout of Your victory. Teach me to fight from redemption, not regret. Let my life thunder with the proof that grace wins. In Jesus' name, Amen.

November 1

"God's grace is not only greater than all our sins, it is also greater than all our circumstances."
Joni Eareckson Tada

Son,
grace isn't just a rescue rope from sin.
It's the sustaining power for every battle, every heartbreak, every obstacle you'll face.

You are not limping through life hoping I'll intervene.
You are running your race fueled by grace stronger than storms and deeper than defeat.

Grace doesn't just cover you when you fall.
It empowers you to stand taller, fight longer, and endure when everything around you says quit.

Don't just survive by grace.
Conquer by grace.

"My grace is sufficient for you, for My power is made perfect in weakness." — 2 Corinthians 12:9

Daily Challenge: In one place you feel weak today, boldly declare: "God's grace is greater than this."

Warrior's Prayer:
Father, I need Your grace not just to forgive but to fuel me. Strengthen my spirit with the unstoppable power of Your mercy. Teach me to rise by Your grace in every battle today. In Jesus' name, Amen.

November 2

*"God is not looking for men of great faith,
but for men ready to follow Him."*
Hudson Taylor

*Son,
you keep waiting until you "feel" more faith.
But faith isn't a feeling.
It's movement.*

*I don't call the fearless.
I call the willing.*

*You don't have to have it all figured out.
You just have to say yes and take the next obedient step.*

*I will meet you on the move.
I will strengthen your faith as you walk.
I will ignite courage once you step into the unknown.*

*Don't sit paralyzed.
Move forward, even if your knees shake.*

"Come, follow Me," Jesus said, "and I will send you out to fish for people." — Matthew 4:19

Daily Challenge: Move forward today in one area where fear has tried to freeze you—trusting that God meets you when you move.

Warrior's Prayer:
Father, I choose obedience over fear today. Strengthen my trembling steps. Meet me in motion. Teach me that following You is the birthplace of faith. I will follow wherever You lead. In Jesus' name, Amen.

November 3

"What God originates, God orchestrates."
Jack Hayford

Son,
you feel the weight
of making it happen.

You think you have to force the door open.
You think you have to control the outcome.

You don't.

What I start,
I sustain.

What I birth,
I build.

You are not the architect of destiny.
You are the obedient carrier of My blueprint.

Trust the Builder.
Trust the Plan-Maker.
Trust the Promise-Keeper.

You are not called to manufacture miracles.
You are called to move faithfully while I orchestrate the impossible.

"He who began a good work in you will carry it on to completion until the day of Christ Jesus."
— Philippians 1:6

Daily Challenge: Surrender today one dream or burden you've been trying to control—and trust God to build it.

Warrior's Prayer:
Father, I trust You to finish what You start. Take the burdens I've tried to carry alone. Teach me to move faithfully while You orchestrate victory. I lay my striving down and lift my eyes to You. In Jesus' name, Amen.

November 4

"The Word of God is the anvil upon which the opinions of men are smashed."
Charles Spurgeon

Son,
the world is loud.
Opinions rage like wildfire.
Truth feels negotiable.
But My Word is still the anvil that shatters every lie.

You were not made to sway with the winds of culture.
You were made to stand on the rock of My Word—unshaken, unashamed, unbreakable.

Anchor your life in Scripture.
Build your battles on My promises.
Let your roots grow deep in truth that cannot be overturned.

When the world shakes, My Word holds.
When opinions clash, My Word stands.

Forge your spirit on the anvil of eternal truth.

"Heaven and earth will pass away, but My words will never pass away." — Matthew 24:35

Daily Challenge: Read and declare a Scripture aloud today over a situation where human opinions have tried to drown out God's voice.

Warrior's Prayer:
Father, anchor me in Your unshakable Word. Let the noise of culture grow silent against the roaring truth of Your promises. Forge my spirit on Your anvil of truth until I am unbreakable in You. In Jesus' name, Amen.

November 5
"The safest place to be is in the center of God's will."
Corrie ten Boom

Son,
safety isn't about the absence of battle.
It's about the presence of My purpose.

You could be surrounded by enemies, standing alone in the crossfire—
and still be safer than a thousand men hiding outside My will.

The center of My will isn't always comfortable.
But it's always invincible.

Move forward boldly, knowing that obedience is your shield.
My plan is your fortress.
My presence is your protection.

Stay in the center, son.
No matter what it costs,
it's the only place worth standing.

> **"The Lord is my light and my salvation—**
> **whom shall I fear?"** — Psalm 27:1

Daily Challenge: Ask God today: "Am I standing fully in the center of Your will?"—then act on what He shows you.

Warrior's Prayer:
Father, position me in the center of Your will and hold me there with fierce obedience. Even when it's costly, teach me that no safer place exists than being fully surrendered to You. Let me fear nothing but drifting from Your side. In Jesus' name, Amen.

November 6

*"God's work done in God's way will
never lack God's supply."*
Hudson Taylor

Son,
you worry about the resources you don't see.
You stress over the numbers, the timing, the odds stacked against you.
But listen—
where I lead, I provide.

Provision follows purpose.
Obedience unlocks supply.
You don't have to be the source—you have to be the vessel.

When you walk in My will, My supply will meet you step for step.
Maybe not early.
Maybe not how you expect.
But always exactly when you need it.

Trust the Provider more than you fear the pressure.

"And my God will meet all your needs according to the riches of His glory in Christ Jesus."
— Philippians 4:19

Daily Challenge: Identify one area you've been anxious about provision—and surrender it to God's supply today.

Warrior's Prayer:
Father, silence the fear that says I have to be my own provider. Teach me to trust Your perfect timing, Your perfect plan, and Your unstoppable supply. I will move forward in obedience, knowing You will meet me there. In Jesus' name, Amen.

November 7

"Our greatest fear should not be of failure, but of succeeding at things in life that don't really matter."
Francis Chan

Son,
you can build an empire and miss eternity.
You can win applause and lose your soul.

The real danger isn't failing.
It's succeeding at things that have no lasting value.

I have called you to build what matters:
Lives transformed.
Souls rescued.
Faith that outlasts every shaking.

Run your race with your eyes locked on the prize that will not fade.
Chase Kingdom victories, not earthly trophies.

Only one Kingdom will stand when the dust settles—build for that.

"But seek first His Kingdom and His righteousness, and all these things will be given to you as well."
— Matthew 6:33

Daily Challenge: Evaluate your top goals today—and make sure at least one of them is a Kingdom goal, not just an earthly one.

Warrior's Prayer:
Father, reset my priorities today. Align my heart with Your eternal Kingdom. Keep me from chasing victories that don't matter in the end. I want my life to count forever, not just for now. In Jesus' name, Amen.

November 8

*"Faith is not belief without proof,
but trust without reservations."*
Elton Trueblood

*Son,
faith is not a gamble.
It's not a desperate hope.
It's a full-throttle trust
in the God who cannot fail.*

*Faith doesn't wait
for the perfect conditions.
Faith doesn't demand
to see the map.
Faith leaps
when logic hesitates.
Faith builds
when others retreat.*

*I am not asking you
to trust a feeling.
I am calling you
to trust My character.*

*Leap.
Build.
Move.*

*No reservations.
No backup plans.
No fear.*

"Now faith is confidence in what we hope for and assurance about what we do not see." — Hebrews 11:1

Daily Challenge: Choose one area today where you've been holding back—and step forward without reservation.

Warrior's Prayer:
Father, grow a faith in me that doesn't flinch, doesn't hesitate, and doesn't require proof before trusting Your heart. Let my life roar with full-throttle faith that terrifies fear. In Jesus' name, Amen.

November 9

"We are all faced with a series of great opportunities brilliantly disguised as impossible situations."
Chuck Swindoll

Son,
your greatest opportunities rarely come dressed as open doors.
They come wrapped in impossibilities.

Battles that look too big.
Mountains that seem unclimbable.
Dreams that feel too crazy.

That's where miracles live.
That's where warriors are made.

Stop seeing obstacles as closed doors.
Start seeing them as invitations for Heaven's power to invade Earth.

Impossible is My favorite playing field.

"For nothing will be impossible with God." — Luke 1:37

Daily Challenge: Identify one situation that looks impossible—and declare today, "This is an opportunity for God's power."

Warrior's Prayer:
Father, open my eyes to the opportunities hidden inside impossibilities. Let me see mountains not as barriers but as stages for Your glory. Teach me to fight with expectation, not intimidation. In Jesus' name, Amen.

November 10
"When I am weak, then I am strong."
2 Corinthians 12:10

Son,
strength isn't the absence of weakness.
Strength is My power roaring through your surrendered heart.

You don't win battles by flexing harder.
You win battles by yielding deeper.

The world despises weakness.
I use it as a gateway to supernatural strength.

When you hit the end of yourself,
you hit the beginning of Me.

Don't be afraid of the places you feel empty—
they are where My Spirit floods in the fullest.

"But He said to me, 'My grace is sufficient for you, for My power is made perfect in weakness.'"
— 2 Corinthians 12:9

Daily Challenge: Lean into an area of weakness today—admit it to God and invite His strength to flood it.

Warrior's Prayer:
Father, I lay my weakness at Your feet without shame. Flood my broken places with Your unstoppable strength. Teach me that Your power shines brightest through my surrendered cracks. In Jesus' name, Amen.

November 11

"You were bought at a price; do not become slaves of men."
1 Corinthians 7:23

Son,
the freedom you walk in today was bought with blood.
The cross proves it.
The battlefield of history shouts it.

Real freedom always costs something—
sacrifice, courage, fierce endurance.

Never forget:
your spiritual freedom cost the blood of the Son of God.
Your ability to live unchained was paid for in full at Calvary.

Freedom isn't a feeling.
It's a reality bought in sacrifice, defended in faith, and lived with purpose.

Honor the cost.
Live worthy of the price.

"It is for freedom that Christ has set us free. Stand firm, then..." — Galatians 5:1

Daily Challenge: Today, thank God deliberately for the freedom you have—and live boldly in it.

Warrior's Prayer:
Father, remind me that my freedom is not cheap. It cost everything. Teach me to live with honor, to fight for what matters, and to walk boldly in the freedom You bought for me with blood. In Jesus' name, Amen.

November 12
"You were made for greatness, not comfort."
Pope Benedict XVI

Son,
comfort will tempt you.
It will whisper that the safe path is the best path.
But comfort zones are killing zones for warriors.

I made you for greatness—
the kind that scars your knees in prayer,
blisters your hands in work,
and stretches your spirit past the breaking point.

You were not made to arrive safely at death.
You were made to storm the gates of hell and leave a mark on eternity.

Choose the hard road today, son.
The narrow road.
The road that few walk but every true hero must.

"Enter through the narrow gate... small is the gate and narrow the road that leads to life, and only a few find it."
— Matthew 7:13–14

Daily Challenge: Step outside your comfort zone today with one action that pushes you toward God's greater calling.

Warrior's Prayer:
Father, crucify my craving for comfort. Call me into the uncomfortable places where real greatness is born. Stretch me. Forge me. Make me into a man who doesn't settle for safe. In Jesus' name, Amen.

November 13

"God's promises are like the stars; the darker the night, the brighter they shine."
David Nicholas

Son,
the night will fall.
The battles will rage.
The shadows will press close.

But lift your eyes, son.

The darker the night,
the louder My promises blaze.

I have not abandoned you.
I have not forgotten you.
I have not changed My word over you.

When the world falls silent,
let My promises be your song.
When the darkness mocks you,
let My promises be your fire.

Hold onto them like swords.
Wield them like shields.
Sing them like war cries.

My promises do not flicker.
They burn brighter when the night falls heavy.

"The grass withers and the flowers fall, but the word of our God endures forever." — Isaiah 40:8

Daily Challenge: Find a specific promise in Scripture today and hold onto it tightly, no matter how you feel.

Warrior's Prayer:
Father, teach me to cling to Your promises when the darkness feels overwhelming. Ignite my faith to burn brighter, not flicker out. Remind me that every word You've spoken will outlast every battle I face. In Jesus' name, Amen.

November 14
"God does not call the qualified; He qualifies the called."
A.W. Tozer

Son,
you may look at your hands and see weakness.
I see weapons.
You may look at your past and see disqualification.
I see preparation.

I don't choose based on resumes.
I choose based on surrender.

If you were enough on your own, you wouldn't need Me.
Your "not enough" is the canvas where My "more than enough" paints masterpieces.

Don't let insecurity silence your calling.
Step forward, even with trembling knees.
I qualify the willing, not the perfect.

"Brothers and sisters, think of what you were when you were called. Not many of you were wise by human standards..." — 1 Corinthians 1:26

Daily Challenge: Step into one area today where you've felt underqualified—and trust God to equip you in motion.

Warrior's Prayer:
Father, I offer You my weakness, my fear, my inexperience. Take my surrendered heart and make it a weapon in Your hand. I trust You to qualify me as I walk. In Jesus' name, Amen.

November 15
"A ship in harbor is safe, but that is not what ships are built for."
John A. Shedd

Son,
you were not crafted to play it safe.
You were not designed to dock forever in the harbor.

The winds were made to fill your sails.
The waves were made to test your mettle.
The oceans of risk were made to reveal the fire inside you.

Safety might feel good for a moment.
But destiny lives out where the waves roar.

You were built for wild obedience, not tame existence.

Launch out, son.
Deep waters await.

"Put out into deep water, and let down the nets for a catch." — Luke 5:4

Daily Challenge: Identify one area where you've been playing it safe—and today, choose to launch deeper in faith.

Warrior's Prayer:
Father, push me out of the harbor of fear. Fill my sails with the winds of faith. Lead me into deep waters where I must depend on You completely. I was made for more than safe living—I was made for bold sailing. In Jesus' name, Amen.

November 16
"He who kneels before God can stand before anyone."
Leonard Ravenhill

Son,
you don't stand strong because of your strength.
You stand strong because of where you kneel.

Kneeling before Me isn't weakness—
it's where warriors are armed with fire.
It's where sons are filled with courage no sword can shatter.

Kneeling is where pride dies and real power is born.
It's where fear evaporates and authority rises.

Kneel low today, son.
Rise invincible.

> **"Humble yourselves before the Lord,**
> **and He will lift you up."**
> — James 4:10

Daily Challenge: Spend time today literally kneeling before God—worship, surrender, and listen.

Warrior's Prayer:
Father, teach me to kneel often and rise unshaken. Strengthen my spirit at Your feet. Break pride, kill fear, and fill me with Heaven's courage as I bow before You. In Jesus' name, Amen.

November 17
"When Christ calls a man, He bids him come and die."
Dietrich Bonhoeffer

Son,
the call to follow Me is not an invitation to comfort—
it's a call to crucifixion.

Die to pride.
Die to fear.
Die to reputation.
Die to every false kingdom that tempts you.

I don't want part of you—I want all of you.

And here's the mystery:
the death I call you to leads to the life you were made for.
Resurrection power waits on the other side of your surrender.

Come and die, son—
and watch Me breathe a fierceness into you that hell can't silence.

"Whoever wants to be My disciple must deny themselves and take up their cross daily and follow Me."
— Luke 9:23

Daily Challenge: Identify one area where your flesh still fights surrender—and lay it fully on the altar today.

Warrior's Prayer:
Father, kill in me everything that competes with You. Teach me that death to self is the doorway to true life. I choose the cross today over comfort. Resurrect in me the warrior You designed. In Jesus' name, Amen.

November 18

*"Hardships often prepare ordinary people for
an extraordinary destiny."*
C.S. Lewis

*Son,
the fire that you fear
is the forge that you need.*

*The crushing weight
is building unbreakable endurance.*

*The breaking
is making.*

*You think hardship is the enemy.
I use it as the training ground of kings.*

*Do not pray away the pressure.
Pray for perseverance.
Do not curse the crushing.
Bless it.*

*Ordinary men
become extraordinary warriors
through unseen battles
and quiet endurance.*

*Stay the course.
The crown is closer than you think.*

"Blessed is the one who perseveres under trial because, having stood the test, that person will receive the crown of life..." — James 1:12

Daily Challenge: Endure hardship today without grumbling—see it as the forge, not the enemy.

Warrior's Prayer:
Father, use the hardship to refine me, not ruin me. Teach me to bless the breaking and embrace the fire. Forge a perseverance in me that no storm can extinguish. In Jesus' name, Amen.

November 19

*"You are never too old to set another goal
or to dream a new dream."*
C.S. Lewis

Son,
there is no expiration date on your calling.
There is no "too late" for the man who walks with Me.

The world will tell you to slow down, settle in, retire your passion.
I tell you to dream bigger, run harder, burn brighter.

I am the God who births new fires in old bones.
I am the God who calls you to fresh battles long after others sit down.

If you're still breathing, you're still dangerous to hell.

Dream again, son.
Rise again.
Fight again.

"They will still bear fruit in old age,
they will stay fresh and green."
— Psalm 92:14

Daily Challenge: Reignite one dream today that fear or failure tried to bury—pray fresh fire into it.

Warrior's Prayer:
Father, breathe fresh dreams into my spirit. Resurrect what I thought was dead. Teach me to dream without limits, run without fear, and fight without quitting. I am never done while You are still moving. In Jesus' name, Amen.

November 20

"You will never know the fullness of Christ until you know the emptiness of everything else."
Charles Spurgeon

Son,
everything else will eventually disappoint you.
Fame fades.
Riches rot.
Praises turn to silence.

But I remain.

You were designed to hunger for something eternal.
Every broken promise of this world is a reminder:
only My fullness can fill you.

Let every shattered dream push you closer to My chest.
Let every fading pleasure drive you deeper into My arms.

I am the only treasure that cannot be taken,
the only joy that cannot be shattered.

"Taste and see that the Lord is good; blessed is the one who takes refuge in Him." — Psalm 34:8

Daily Challenge: Spend quiet time today asking God to strip away anything you're using to fill the place only He should have.

Warrior's Prayer:
Father, empty my hands of every counterfeit treasure. Teach me that You alone satisfy the deepest hunger of my soul. Fill me today with the fullness that only comes from Your presence. In Jesus' name, Amen.

November 21
"Gratitude turns what we have into enough."
Melody Beattie

Son,
the enemy will tempt you to live hungry for more—
more recognition, more achievement, more approval.
But gratitude arms you with fierce contentment.

Gratitude is not weakness.
It's rebellion against the lie that you are lacking.

When you thank Me, you fight back against entitlement.
When you thank Me, you shatter fear and fertilize faith.

You are richer than you realize.
You are already standing in fields of blessing.

Open your eyes today.
Gratitude is your greatest weapon.

> **"Give thanks in all circumstances; for this is God's will for you in Christ Jesus."**
> — 1 Thessalonians 5:18

Daily Challenge: Speak aloud five specific things you're thankful for today—and let gratitude fuel your strength.

Warrior's Prayer:
Father, open my eyes to see the ocean of blessings around me. Let gratitude become my war cry against fear, envy, and entitlement. Teach me that enough is found not in having more, but in seeing You more clearly. In Jesus' name, Amen.

November 22

*"When you choose to forgive those who have hurt you,
you take away their power."*
Lewis B. Smedes

Son,
forgiveness is not letting someone off the hook.
It's letting yourself off the chain.

Unforgiveness is a prison you lock from the inside.
It drains your strength, poisons your peace, and distracts
you from your calling.

Forgiveness doesn't deny the pain.
It declares that the pain will not rule you.

Forgiveness takes the knife out of your heart
and places the wounds into My healing hands.

Release them, son.
Not because they deserve it—
but because you deserve freedom.

"Forgive as the Lord forgave you." — Colossians 3:13

Daily Challenge: Forgive someone today—even if it's just between you and God—and walk lighter.

Warrior's Prayer:
Father, I release the weight of bitterness and unforgiveness. I choose to forgive as You forgave me—freely, fiercely, fully. Heal my wounds and free my spirit to fight with a whole heart. In Jesus' name, Amen.

November 23

"You have as much laughter as you have faith."
Martin Luther

Son,
faith and fear cannot breathe the same air.

Faith laughs in the face of storms.
Faith sings while chains rattle.
Faith stands tall
while the world trembles.

You were not made to walk through life grim and crushed.
You were made to walk with joy flaming in your spirit,
even when the battle rages.

Laugh, son—
not because life is easy,
but because you know who wins.

Laugh because the King is on the throne.
Laugh because no darkness can put out your light.

Faith laughs louder than fear.

"The joy of the Lord is your strength." — Nehemiah 8:10

Daily Challenge: Laugh today—deliberately. Choose joy even in tension. Let laughter be a declaration of faith.

Warrior's Prayer:
Father, reignite laughter and joy in my spirit today. Teach me that joy is not weakness—it's a weapon. Let my laughter roar louder than fear, and let my faith light fires even in dark places. In Jesus' name, Amen.

November 24

"Faith is deliberate confidence in the character of God whose ways you may not understand at the time."
Oswald Chambers

Son,
you won't always understand My ways.
But you can always trust My heart.

Faith is not built on having all the answers.
Faith is built on knowing Me enough to move forward without them.

When the road twists,
when the answers are delayed,
when the prayers seem unanswered—
anchor yourself in My character, not in your circumstances.

I have never failed.
I am not about to start with you.

Trust Me, even in the shadows.

"Trust in the Lord with all your heart and lean not on your own understanding." — Proverbs 3:5

Daily Challenge: In one situation where you don't understand God's timing or answer—declare today, "I trust Your heart even when I don't see Your hand."

Warrior's Prayer:
Father, teach me to trust You deeper than my need to understand. Anchor me in Your goodness when answers seem delayed. Let my faith be fierce because my confidence is in Your unchanging heart. In Jesus' name, Amen.

November 25
"God never said the journey would be easy, but He did say the arrival would be worthwhile."
Max Lucado

Son,
the road is rugged.
The climb is brutal.
The battle bruises.

But don't let the hardness make you doubt the promise.

The fight is fierce because the prize is glorious.
The wounds are deep because the reward is eternal.

You were not promised ease—you were promised victory.
You were not promised comfort—you were promised a crown.

Keep marching, son.
The finish line is closer than you think.
And Heaven's roar will make every battle worth it.

"I have fought the good fight, I have finished the race, I have kept the faith." — 2 Timothy 4:7

Daily Challenge: Today, when you feel weary, whisper aloud: "It's hard—but it's worth it."

Warrior's Prayer:
Father, when the road feels endless, lift my eyes to the reward You promised. Strengthen my steps when I want to stop. Help me finish this race not with regret, but with fire in my spirit and victory in my hands. In Jesus' name, Amen.

November 26
"Prayer is not overcoming God's reluctance.
It is laying hold of His willingness."
Martin Luther

Son,
when you pray, you're not trying to twist My arm.
You're stepping into the willingness of Heaven.
I am not reluctant to bless you.
I am not hesitant to move.

I am more ready to answer than you are to ask.
I am more ready to pour out than you are to receive.

Prayer isn't convincing Me.
Prayer is connecting to Me.

Lay hold of My promises, son.
Lay hold of My willingness.
Pray like a warrior pulling Heaven into earth.

"Ask and it will be given to you; seek and you will find; knock and the door will be opened to you."
— Matthew 7:7

Daily Challenge: Pray boldly today for something you've hesitated to ask for—and trust God's heart to answer.

Warrior's Prayer:
Father, teach me to pray with boldness, not timidity. Remind me that You are more willing to bless than I am to ask. Let my prayers be fierce, faith-filled, and grounded in Your unstoppable goodness. In Jesus' name, Amen.

November 27

"You have never tested God's resources until you have attempted the impossible."
F.B. Meyer

Son,
safe dreams don't need supernatural supply.
Tame prayers don't need Heaven's armies.

I am calling you into deeper waters—
where your resources aren't enough,
where your strength runs out,
where your only hope is Me.

Faith flourishes when fear says it's impossible.
Miracles multiply where logic gives up.

Test the depth of My resources, son.
Attempt the impossible.
And watch Me pour out what you could never earn, build, or deserve.

> **"With man this is impossible, but with God all things are possible."**
> — Matthew 19:26

Daily Challenge: Attempt something today that feels beyond your strength—and trust God to meet you there.

Warrior's Prayer:
Father, I choose to dream bigger and pray louder today. Stretch my faith past my comfort zone. Teach me to test the endless resources of Your Kingdom through bold obedience. In Jesus' name, Amen.

November 28

*"The Lord gives His hardest battles to
His strongest soldiers."*
Charles Spurgeon

Son,
the size of your battle
is not a sign of your failure.

It's a sign of your strength.

The enemy would not attack you so fiercely
if you weren't a threat.

The darkness would not press so hard
if your light wasn't breaking through.

I trust you with battles
because I have already filled you with My strength.

You are not abandoned.
You are armed.

You are not overwhelmed.
You are an overcomer.

Fight, son.
The battle is proof you are advancing.

"The Lord is a warrior; the Lord is His name."
— Exodus 15:3

Daily Challenge: When the battle feels heavy today, say this aloud: "This is proof I'm advancing."

Warrior's Prayer:
Father, teach me to see battles as evidence of breakthrough. Remind me that if I were not dangerous to the enemy, he would not attack so fiercely. Fill me with the warrior spirit of Heaven today. In Jesus' name, Amen.

November 29

*"The greatness of a man's power is the
measure of his surrender."*
William Booth

Son,
real power is not found in holding on.
It's found in letting go.

The world teaches you to clench your fists tighter.
I call you to open your hands wider.

You gain strength by surrender.
You gain influence by submission.
You gain authority by laying your crown at My feet.

The men who have changed history for My glory
have always been the ones who surrendered deepest.

Surrender is not your defeat—it is your destiny.

"Submit yourselves, then, to God. Resist the devil, and he will flee from you." — James 4:7

Daily Challenge: Spend five minutes today surrendering specific fears, dreams, and burdens to God—out loud.

Warrior's Prayer:
Father, teach me to win by surrender. Crush the pride that clings to control. Fill my open hands with weapons stronger than fear, shame, or pride. I choose to kneel so I can rise in Your strength. In Jesus' name, Amen.

November 30
"Only one life, 'twill soon be past; only what's done for Christ will last."
C.T. Studd

Son,
your life is a mist—
a vapor that will vanish faster than you think.

The trophies of this world will tarnish.
The praises of man will fade into silence.
The kingdoms built by flesh will crumble into dust.

But everything done for Me will outlive the stars.

Live today with eternity echoing in your spirit.
Measure success not by the size of your bank account,
but by the size of your obedience.

Only what's done for Christ will stand when everything else burns.

"The world and its desires pass away, but whoever does the will of God lives forever." — 1 John 2:17

Daily Challenge: Examine one major goal in your life today—and ask: "Will this still matter in eternity?"

Warrior's Prayer:
Father, stamp eternity on my eyes. Teach me to invest my strength in what will never fade. Let me build, fight, and love with forever in mind—not just today. Make my life echo through eternity. In Jesus' name, Amen.

December 1

"The beginning of anxiety is the end of faith, and the beginning of true faith is the end of anxiety."
George Müller

Son,
faith and anxiety cannot rule your heart at the same time.
One will rise. One will fall.

Anxiety demands you obsess over what might happen.
Faith declares victory over what will happen.

Anxiety shrinks your spirit.
Faith expands your soul.

Feed faith—and anxiety starves.
Feed fear—and faith weakens.

Choose your diet carefully today.
Let faith be your feast.

"Cast all your anxiety on Him because He cares for you."
— 1 Peter 5:7

Daily Challenge: The moment anxiety rises today, say aloud: "I cast this on You, Lord. I choose faith."

Warrior's Prayer:
Father, teach me to starve fear and feed faith. Help me to throw every anxious thought onto Your mighty shoulders. Fill me today with peace that shouts louder than my fears. In Jesus' name, Amen.

December 2

"The Spirit of God first imparts love; He next inspires hope, and then gives liberty; and these are always attended by humility."
Charles Spurgeon

Son,
love fuels your battles.
Hope lifts your shield.
Liberty strengthens your feet.

And humility keeps it all pure.

Without humility, your gifts rot into pride.
Without humility, your victories twist into trophies for your ego.

Stay low before Me, son.
Stay desperate for My presence.
Stay small in your own eyes.

Because the lower you kneel,
the higher I lift you.

"God opposes the proud but gives grace to the humble."
— 1 Peter 5:5

Daily Challenge: Find a way today to intentionally honor someone else's victory instead of craving recognition for your own.

Warrior's Prayer:
Father, keep my heart soft, my spirit humble, and my eyes fixed on You. Remind me that Your grace flows where pride cannot live. I kneel low so You can be lifted high through me. In Jesus' name, Amen.

December 3

"I have held many things in my hands, and I have lost them all; but whatever I have placed in God's hands, that I still possess."
Martin Luther

Son,
tight fists lose the most.

Grip your dreams too tightly,
and they slip like sand.
Grip your treasures too fiercely,
and they rot in your grasp.

But open hands
never lose.

Everything you place in My hands—
your dreams, your battles, your relationships—
is secured beyond rust, loss, and death.

Release your grip, son.
Place it all in My scarred hands.
What you give to Me,
you never truly lose.

"Commit your way to the Lord; trust in Him and He will do this." — Psalm 37:5

Daily Challenge: Physically open your hands today as you pray—and surrender one thing you've been trying to control.

Warrior's Prayer:
Father, I open my hands today. I place my battles, my blessings, my future into Yours. Take them, hold them, guard them. I trust Your hands far more than I trust my own. In Jesus' name, Amen.

December 4

"Faith sees the invisible, believes the unbelievable, and receives the impossible."
Corrie ten Boom

Son,
the world says, "See it, then believe it."
I say, "Believe it—and you will see it."

Faith has eyes stronger than fear.
Faith builds bridges where others only see cliffs.

You are not bound by what you can see.
You are fueled by what I have spoken.

Walk forward, son—
even if the road looks invisible.
Even if the odds seem impossible.

Faith sees what the eyes cannot.

"For we live by faith, not by sight." — 2 Corinthians 5:7

Daily Challenge: Take one step of obedience today that doesn't make logical sense but is fueled by faith.

Warrior's Prayer:
Father, sharpen my spiritual vision. Teach me to walk by Your promises, not my sight. Strengthen my faith to believe for what I cannot yet see—and to move boldly toward it. In Jesus' name, Amen.

December 5
"We are immortal until our work is done."
George Whitefield

Son,
your life is not ruled by chance.
Your days are not at the mercy of fate.

Your mission is sealed by My hand.
Your time is held by My sovereignty.

No sickness, no enemy, no failure can take you out before My purpose in you is complete.

So live bold.
Love deeply.
Fight fiercely.

You are immortal until the last chapter I wrote for you is finished.

"I have fought the good fight, I have finished the race, I have kept the faith." — 2 Timothy 4:7

Daily Challenge: Live today with boldness—as if you are unstoppable until God's purpose is complete (because you are).

Warrior's Prayer:
Father, let me live with fearless faith today. Teach me that my life is held in Your sovereign hands. Until my race is finished, I will fight with boldness, love with passion, and move without fear. In Jesus' name, Amen.

December 6

"The will of God will not take you where the grace of God cannot sustain you."
Billy Graham

Son,
the road I call you to may be steep.
The rivers may rise.
The fires may rage.

But My grace is not a maybe—
it's a guarantee.

If I lead you to it,
I will fuel you through it.

You will not run out.
You will not be abandoned.
You will not be crushed beyond My rescue.

Trust that wherever I send you,
I have already paved the way with sustaining strength.

"My grace is sufficient for you, for My power is made perfect in weakness." — 2 Corinthians 12:9

Daily Challenge: When today feels overwhelming, whisper this out loud: "God's grace is my fuel."

Warrior's Prayer:
Father, anchor my confidence in Your sustaining grace. Remind me that no battle, no burden, no calling will outpace Your provision. I walk forward today carried by Your unbreakable strength. In Jesus' name, Amen.

December 7

*"Holiness is not the way to Christ;
Christ is the way to holiness."*
Adrian Rogers

Son,
you don't earn My presence by getting everything right.
You pursue holiness because you are already mine.

Religion says, "Perform to be loved."
I say, "Because you are loved, walk differently."

Holiness isn't drudgery—it's freedom.
Holiness isn't chains—it's a war cry.
Holiness isn't about perfection—it's about pursuit.

Chase My heart first.
Holiness will follow.

> **"But just as He who called you is holy,
> so be holy in all you do."**
> — 1 Peter 1:15

Daily Challenge: Choose today to pursue holiness not out of fear, but out of fierce gratitude for being loved.

Warrior's Prayer:
Father, teach me that holiness is not a burden but a battlefield I get to fight from victory. Let my life reflect the freedom and passion of a heart fully set apart for You. In Jesus' name, Amen.

December 8

"You can give without loving, but you cannot love without giving."
Amy Carmichael

Son,
love that does not move
is not love.

Real love
gets dirt under its fingernails.
Real love
bleeds, sweats, gives.

You cannot claim love
and stay passive.

Love pours out.
Love steps up.
Love lays down its rights
for the sake of another's rescue.

If you would love,
you must give.
Not just from your wallet—
but from your heart,
your strength,
your dreams.

The love that costs you nothing
is worth nothing.

"Greater love has no one than this: to lay down one's life for one's friends." — John 15:13

Daily Challenge: Look for one opportunity today to love someone sacrificially—whether it's inconvenient, costly, or unnoticed.

Warrior's Prayer:
Father, ignite a love in me that is not safe or selfish but fierce and sacrificial. Teach me that love is proven not in words but in wounds willingly carried. Make me a warrior who loves like You. In Jesus' name, Amen.

December 9

"Peace is not the absence of trouble,
but the presence of Christ."
Sheila Walsh

Son,
peace isn't when the battle ends.
Peace is when you remember who rides with you through the battle.

My presence is your anchor in the middle of the hurricane.
My voice is your stillness when chaos screams.

Don't wait for circumstances to calm down.
Anchor yourself now.

When you carry My presence,
you carry an unshakable fortress wherever you go.

"The Lord gives strength to His people; the Lord blesses His people with peace." — Psalm 29:11

Daily Challenge: In one moment of stress today, stop and say: "I carry the presence of Christ—I have peace now."

Warrior's Prayer:
Father, let Your peace rule my heart today. Remind me that true peace is not the absence of war, but the presence of Your victory. Anchor me in the stillness that only You provide. In Jesus' name, Amen.

December 10
"Good is not always God's best."
Oswald Chambers

Son,
not everything urgent is important.
Not everything loud deserves your attention.

The enemy loves to distract warriors with noise,
busywork,
pointless battles.

Stay locked on the mission.
Don't let distractions pull you from destiny.

It takes strength to say no.
It takes focus to stay on the wall when others call you down.

You are not called to do everything.
You are called to do what matters most.

"But I focus on this one thing: Forgetting the past and looking forward to what lies ahead."
— Philippians 3:13

Daily Challenge: Identify one distraction you need to cut today—and refocus on the mission God has given you.

Warrior's Prayer:
Father, sharpen my focus today. Teach me to say no to distractions and yes to destiny. Give me the courage to walk away from what is merely good so I can chase what is vital. I choose mission over noise. In Jesus' name, Amen.

December 11

"Don't pray when you feel like it. Have an appointment with the Lord and keep it."
Corrie ten Boom

Son,
feelings make a terrible foundation.
Discipline builds legacy.

You don't go to war when you feel like it—
you go because the mission matters.
Prayer is your war room,
your supply line,
your shield maintenance.

Don't let feelings lead you.
Let faithfulness drive you.

Warriors don't wait for comfort to connect—
they show up daily,
knees down,
hands open,
heart ready.

Your consistency will shape your destiny.

"Very early in the morning... Jesus got up, left the house and went off to a solitary place, where He prayed."
— Mark 1:35

Daily Challenge: Set a specific time to meet with God today—and keep that appointment like your life depends on it.

Warrior's Prayer:
Father, make me a man of consistent connection. When my feelings fail, let my discipline stand. Build in me a war-room rhythm that keeps me close to Your heart and sharp for every battle. In Jesus' name, Amen.

December 12
"The greatest battles are won when no one is watching."
Charles Spurgeon

Son,
what you do in secret
is what defines you in the spotlight.

Private surrender
precedes public strength.
Private repentance
precedes public anointing.

The most dangerous warriors
are forged in silence,
where no applause echoes,
but My eyes see every move.

Don't chase platform.
Chase purity.

I will reward what's done in the quiet with power that shakes the earth.

"Then your Father, who sees what is done in secret, will reward you." — Matthew 6:6

Daily Challenge: Choose today to serve, give, or obey in a secret way—just between you and God.

Warrior's Prayer:
Father, remind me that the secret place is where the real battle is won. Make my private life a fortress of faith, obedience, and purity. Let me be faithful in silence so I can carry strength in public. In Jesus' name, Amen.

December 13
"The future is as bright as the promises of God."
William Carey

Son,
you look ahead
and see fog,
fear,
unknowns.

But I see fields of fire,
harvest,
victory.

Your future is not shaped
by the world's chaos.
It is anchored in My covenant.

Do not be afraid of what's next.
Be expectant.

I go before you.
My promises light the path.
My presence never leaves.

Don't stare into the shadows—
walk into the light I've already spoken over you.

"For I know the plans I have for you... plans to give you a hope and a future." — Jeremiah 29:11

Daily Challenge: Declare this today over your next season: "My future is forged by God's promises—not my fear."

Warrior's Prayer:
Father, I trust You with tomorrow. Burn Your promises into my spirit. Teach me to look ahead not with anxiety, but with the confidence of a son led by a faithful King. In Jesus' name, Amen.

December 14

"Don't shine so others can see you. Shine so that through you, others can see Him."
C.S. Lewis

Son,
this world loves to spotlight.
But I've called you to reflect.

You are not the fire.
You are the torch.
You are not the source.
You are the vessel.

Shine not to be seen,
but so others can see Me through you.

Your greatest power isn't in your presence—
it's in My presence flowing through your obedience.

Let every success point to the Savior.
Let every victory glorify the Victor.

"Let your light shine before others, that they may see your good deeds and glorify your Father in heaven."
— Matthew 5:16

Daily Challenge: In one conversation or action today, make it a point to redirect honor to God.

Warrior's Prayer:
Father, burn away any craving for spotlight in me. Let my life reflect Your glory, not mine. May others see Your fire through my faithfulness. I want to shine for You alone. In Jesus' name, Amen.

December 15

*"When I cannot read, when I cannot think, when
I cannot even pray, I can trust."*
Hudson Taylor

Son,
some days will feel like silence.
You won't have the words.
You won't feel the fire.
You may even feel numb.

But in the silence, trust.
When you can't climb—cling.
When you can't speak—stand.
When you can't move—hold.

Your strength isn't proven in your noise—
it's proven in your trust.

I am still God in the quiet.
I am still good when the fire dies down.
Your trust is louder than a thousand prayers when spoken in faith.

"Though He slay me, yet will I hope in Him."
— Job 13:15

Daily Challenge: When you feel spiritually dry today, don't run—sit with God in the silence and simply say, "I still trust You."

Warrior's Prayer:
Father, when my words run out, let my trust remain. Teach me that silence is not separation. Anchor my soul in Your presence even when I can't feel it. I trust You, even in the stillness. In Jesus' name, Amen.

December 16

"To be a Christian means to forgive the inexcusable because God has forgiven the inexcusable in you."
C.S. Lewis

Son,
forgiveness isn't optional.
It's warfare.

Bitterness is a quiet assassin—
it hardens your heart,
dims your vision,
and handcuffs your calling.

You weren't called to carry wounds—
you were called to release them.
You weren't built to store rage—
you were built to walk in freedom.

The cross doesn't just cleanse you—
it frees you to forgive.

Let go, son.
Not because they deserve it—
but because I've set you free.

"Forgive, and you will be forgiven." — Luke 6:37

Daily Challenge: Forgive today. Not because it's easy, but because your soul was made to live unchained.

Warrior's Prayer:
Father, I choose to forgive. I lay down every offense, every scar, and every grudge at Your feet. Teach me to walk in the freedom I've been given, and never carry chains that Christ already broke. In Jesus' name, Amen.

December 17

"If Jesus isn't Lord of all, He isn't Lord at all."
Vance Havner

Son,
partial surrender is full rebellion.
I will not take second place in your heart.

I'm not interested in your leftovers.
I'm not impressed by your Sunday face while your private life rots.

I want every room.
Every thought.
Every ambition.
Every desire.

Total surrender is not weakness—
it is the only doorway to real power.

I cannot fill what you won't fully open.

"Love the Lord your God with all your heart and with all your soul and with all your mind." — Matthew 22:37

Daily Challenge: Ask God today: "Is there any part of my life I haven't fully surrendered?" Then act on what He shows you.

Warrior's Prayer:
Father, take it all. No more compartments. No more negotiations. I give You every corner of my life—public and private, seen and unseen. Be Lord of all. In Jesus' name, Amen.

December 18

"We have all eternity to celebrate our victories, but only a few short hours before sunset to win them."
Amy Carmichael

Son,
time is short.
This breath is not a rehearsal.

You don't get forever
to fight.
To lead.
To love.
To burn with holy fire.

Do not waste the daylight.

The battles you dodge today
become the regrets of tomorrow.

The calls you ignore
become the echoes that haunt.

You have this hour.
This fight.
This mission.

Win it.
Don't delay.
Don't drift.

The sun is setting—
fight while there's still fire in your lungs.

"Teach us to number our days, that we may gain a heart of wisdom." — Psalm 90:12

Daily Challenge: Take action today on something eternal you've been delaying—don't wait another moment.

Warrior's Prayer:
Father, burn urgency into my bones. Teach me to seize each moment as if eternity depends on it. I will not waste this day—I will fight with everything I've got. In Jesus' name, Amen.

December 19

"I am not afraid of failure; I am afraid of succeeding at things that don't matter."
William Carey

Son,
hell doesn't always come at you with destruction—
sometimes it comes with distraction.

You were not made to win meaningless trophies.
You were made to carry Kingdom weight.

Busyness is not fruitfulness.
Success is not obedience.

You could build an empire
and miss your assignment.
You could gain the world
and lose your soul.

Fix your eyes, son.
Focus your fire.
Run for what lasts.

"What good is it for someone to gain the whole world, yet forfeit their soul?" — Mark 8:36

Daily Challenge: Audit your goals today—and make sure they reflect eternal purpose, not just temporary success.

Warrior's Prayer:
Father, don't let me waste my strength on things that don't matter. Sharpen my focus. Realign my aim. Let my life be aimed at eternity—not applause. In Jesus' name, Amen.

December 20

*"God uses men who are weak and feeble
enough to lean on Him."*
Hudson Taylor

Son,
I don't need your strength.
I need your surrender.

I use men who know they can't win without Me.
Men who fight on their knees.
Men who cry out when the world says "stay strong."

Your weakness is not a liability—
it's a doorway.

When you lean on Me,
you stand taller.
When you fall into Me,
you rise stronger.

Dependence isn't failure.
It's fuel.

"When I am weak, then I am strong."
— 2 Corinthians 12:10

Daily Challenge: In one area today where you feel weak—lean in, don't fake it. Declare: "Lord, I need You here."

Warrior's Prayer:
Father, I am not ashamed of my weakness—I hand it to You. Let my need be the place Your power explodes through me. I lean hard into You today. You are my strength. In Jesus' name, Amen.

December 21
"You may choose to look the other way, but you can never say again that you did not know."
William Wilberforce

Son,
you weren't born to turn your head.
You weren't saved to stay silent.

You are not responsible for every battle—
but you are responsible for how you respond to what you see.

When injustice screams,
when the weak are crushed,
when truth is buried under comfort—
you must rise.

Warriors don't watch.
They step in.
They speak up.
They fight for what matters.

Look around.
Then act.

"Speak up for those who cannot speak for themselves, for the rights of all who are destitute."
— Proverbs 31:8

Daily Challenge: Choose to take action today—speak, serve, or stand—for someone who can't fight for themselves.

Warrior's Prayer:
Father, I won't close my eyes to brokenness. Give me boldness to act, not just observe. Teach me to carry courage into dark places and be the voice for the voiceless. In Jesus' name, Amen.

December 22

*"He is no fool who gives what he cannot keep
to gain what he cannot lose."*
Jim Elliot

Son,
this world is fading.
Every treasure you cling to here
is slipping through your fingers.

But I offer something eternal.
Something fireproof.
Something death can't touch.

Lay down what won't last
to gain what never ends.

Don't waste your life preserving comfort.
Spend it pursuing purpose.
The greatest trades always look foolish to those who don't
see eternity.

You are not a fool for giving everything—
you are a fool if you don't.

"Whoever loses their life for Me will find it."
— Matthew 16:25

Daily Challenge: Let go of one thing today that's holding you back from full surrender—something temporary for something eternal.

Warrior's Prayer:
Father, I surrender what I cannot keep to gain what I cannot lose. Teach me to trade comfort for calling. Let my life echo with the wisdom of sacrifice. In Jesus' name, Amen.

December 23
"Joy is the serious business of Heaven."
C.S. Lewis

Son,
joy is not a decoration.
It is a weapon.

Not a seasonal feeling—
but a spiritual force
that hell cannot crush.

Joy sings in prisons.
Joy rises in grief.
Joy stands unshaken
because it knows the war has already been won.

Don't wait for joy to find you—
fight for it.

Joy isn't pretending everything's okay.
It's knowing that even if it's not—
God still is.

"The joy of the Lord is your strength." — Nehemiah 8:10

Daily Challenge: Choose joy today in one situation where it doesn't make sense—and let it change the atmosphere.

Warrior's Prayer:
Father, fill me with unshakable joy today. Not based on outcomes, but anchored in Your victory. Let joy rise like a battle cry and fuel my fight through every trial. In Jesus' name, Amen.

December 24
*"The Son of God became a man to enable
men to become sons of God."*
C.S. Lewis

Son,
this is what Christmas means:
Heaven invaded earth
so you could come home.

The manger was not a decoration—
it was a declaration of war.
God with us.
God for us.
God inside of us.

The incarnation was My battle strategy—
to rescue you not from a distance,
but from within.

You are not forgotten.
You are not just a number.
You are My son, purchased with blood, born again through fire.

Celebrate not with sentiment—
but with sacred wonder.

> **"The Word became flesh and made His dwelling among us."** — John 1:14

Daily Challenge: Reflect today not just on Christ's birth—but on your rebirth through Him. Celebrate with awe.

Warrior's Prayer:
Father, thank You for sending Jesus—not just to visit but to save. Let the wonder of His birth ignite fresh fire in my spirit today. I live because He came. In Jesus' name, Amen.

December 25
"Christ was born in the first century,
but He belongs to all centuries."
J.I. Packer

Son,
today the world celebrates with lights and gifts—
but never forget:
the real gift was a war cry in the womb of a virgin.

Jesus didn't come to decorate the season—
He came to decimate darkness.

He came not just to bring peace—
but to crush the serpent's head.
To bring sons and daughters home.
To ignite resurrection in dead hearts.

This is your King.
This is your banner.
This is the beginning of your victory.

Rejoice today—
not with surface-level joy,
but with the deep roar of a warrior redeemed.

"Today in the town of David a Savior has been born to you; He is the Messiah, the Lord." — Luke 2:11

Daily Challenge: Celebrate today not just with tradition—but with fire. Worship like a man who's been rescued.

Warrior's Prayer:
Jesus, You are my King. You came not just to be born, but to battle—and to win. Let my life today be a celebration of the victory You secured. Light a fresh fire in me. In Your name, Amen.

December 26

"The man who mobilizes the Christian church to pray will make the greatest contribution to world evangelization in history."
Andrew Murray

Son,
you don't change the world through louder opinions—
you change it through deeper intercession.

Prayer is not a backup plan.
It's a front-line assault.
It is power wrapped in surrender,
fire fueled by dependence.

If you want to see revival,
start by igniting the altar in your own heart.

Your prayers move armies.
Your prayers shake nations.
Your prayers matter more than you know.

"The prayer of a righteous person is powerful and effective." — James 5:16

Daily Challenge: Spend intentional, focused time interceding for revival today—your family, your city, your nation.

Warrior's Prayer:
Father, ignite intercession in me. Teach me to carry the burdens of others into Your presence and war for them on my knees. Let my prayers be arrows of fire that strike the heart of heaven. In Jesus' name, Amen.

December 27
"You are the only Bible some unbelievers will ever read."
John MacArthur

Son,
your words matter.
But your life shouts louder.

The way you walk, love, suffer, and stand—
it preaches.

There are eyes watching you who won't step into a church,
but they're watching the sermon of your life.

Let them see strength through surrender.
Let them see truth without compromise.
Let them see Jesus in how you show up when it's hard.

You may be the only glimpse of My heart they ever get.
Live it well, son.
Live it real.

"Let your light shine before others, that they may see your good deeds and glorify your Father in heaven."
— Matthew 5:16

Daily Challenge: Ask God to show you one person who's watching your life—and live with intentionality today to reflect Him clearly.

Warrior's Prayer:
Father, let my life preach louder than any words. Teach me to reflect You in everything—in trials, victories, and quiet moments. May those around me see You clearly through the way I live. In Jesus' name, Amen.

December 28

"There is no pit so deep that God's love is not deeper still."
Corrie ten Boom

Son,
you may walk through valleys
that echo with silence.
You may sink in pits
where hope feels like myth.

But I am deeper still.

Deeper than regret.
Deeper than failure.
Deeper than the wounds
you've never dared speak aloud.

I will not let you drown
in what I died to redeem.

There is no darkness
that can outmatch My light.

Lift your eyes, son.
I am already in the pit with you—
lifting you out.

"He lifted me out of the slimy pit, out of the mud and mire; He set my feet on a rock..." — Psalm 40:2

Daily Challenge: Reflect today on one pit God has rescued you from—and thank Him with bold praise.

Warrior's Prayer:
Father, thank You for reaching into the places no one else could. Thank You for finding me, lifting me, restoring me. I will not live in shame—I will live as a son set free. In Jesus' name, Amen.

December 29

*"What you do every day matters more than
what you do once in a while."*
Tim Keller

*Son,
your legacy isn't built in the spotlight—
it's built in the daily grind.*

*One decision.
One act of obedience.
One quiet yes after another.*

*Greatness is formed in repetition.
In consistency.
In showing up when no one claps.*

*Don't chase the flash.
Chase faithfulness.*

*The man who wins the long war
is the one who keeps swinging
when others stop.*

**"Let us not become weary in doing good, for at the
proper time we will reap a harvest if we
do not give up."** — Galatians 6:9

Daily Challenge: Double down today on one habit of faithfulness you've been building—commit to consistency over hype.

Warrior's Prayer:
Father, help me stay consistent. Teach me to value daily faithfulness more than occasional bursts. Let my life become a long obedience in the same direction. In Jesus' name, Amen.

December 30

*"Courage is contagious. When a brave man takes a stand,
the spines of others are often stiffened."*
Billy Graham

Son,
you've been saved for more than survival.
You've been called to holy risk.

Don't play it safe.
Don't shrink your prayers.
Don't bury your dreams in the name of caution.

You carry My Spirit.
You walk with resurrection power.
So live like it.

Attempt things that require miracles.
Expect results only I can deliver.
The world needs more men who are not afraid to dream dangerously.

You were born to push the Kingdom forward.

"Now to Him who is able to do immeasurably more than all we ask or imagine..." — Ephesians 3:20

Daily Challenge: Attempt something today that requires God to show up—pray, act, or speak with boldness.

Warrior's Prayer:
Father, expand my vision. Give me courage to step out of comfort and into the calling. May I never settle for safety when You've called me to faith. Let my life be marked by bold obedience. In Jesus' name, Amen.

December 31

"I have no regrets. I've lived the life God gave me."
Billy Graham

Son,
when the dust settles,
the applause fades,
and your story nears its final chapter—
what will echo in eternity
is not what you built,
but who you became.

I want you to finish empty—
poured out,
fired up,
unapologetically faithful.

Don't die with dreams buried.
Don't die with obedience delayed.
Finish this race like a warrior.

Live loud.
Love well.
Fight clean.
Stand tall.

And when the trumpet sounds,
you'll hear the only words that matter—
"Well done."

"I have fought the good fight, I have finished the race, I have kept the faith." — 2 Timothy 4:7

Daily Challenge: Reflect on the year. Write down what God has done—and what you're still willing to give Him in the year ahead.

Warrior's Prayer:
Father, thank You for walking with me every step of this year. Thank You for the battles, the growth, the scars, and the victories. As I finish this year, I recommit my whole life to You. Make me a warrior that finishes well. In Jesus' name, Amen.

MISSION COMPLETE

But the war isn't over…

You've just completed 365 days of spiritual war plans.
That's not just an achievement- it's a declaration.
A year of showing up. A year of discipline, surrender, obedience, and grit. A year of refusing to live passive, lukewarm, or defeated. But this isn't the end.

You were never called to finish strong for a moment. You were called to live strong for a lifetime.

This devotional was a foundation. Now it's time to build higher. If this journey impacted you, don't stop here.

The Soulcon Series was written to fuel the next steps of your growth as a warrior of God. Head over to Amazon and explore the rest of the Soulcon Series including:

- Soulcon Challenge
- Soulcon Warrior Elite
- Soulcon Operator (soulconchallenge.com)

Thousands of men across the world are rising daily, shoulder-to-shoulder in brotherhood, courage, and Kingdom purpose. You're not alone. You're not finished. You were born for more.

I'm proud of you and I want to encourage you keep fighting to advance the Kingdom every single day until the trumpet sounds, or our bodies run out of life.

Love you guys,

Cody Bobay

DOWNLOAD THE SOULCON APP TODAY
CONTINUE THE SOULCON
WARRIOR LIFESTYLE

Printed in Great Britain
by Amazon